for 11 - 14s

BOOK 6

CHRISTIAN FOCUS PUBLICATIONS

We believe that the Bible is God's word to mankind, and that it contains everything we need to know in order to be reconciled with God and live in a way that is pleasing to him. Therefore, we believe it is vital to teach young teens accurately from the Bible, being careful to teach each passage's true meaning in an appropriate way for the age group, rather than selecting a 'teen's message' from a Biblical passage.

© TnT Ministries
29 Buxton Gardens, Acton, London, W3 9LE
Tel: +44 (0)20 8992 0450 Fax: +44 (0)20 8896 1847
e-mail: sales@tntministries.org.uk

Published in 2003 by Christian Focus Publications Ltd.
Geanies House, Fearn, Tain, Ross-shire, IV20 1TW
Tel: +44 (0)1862 871 011 Fax: +44 (0)1862 871 699
e-mail: **info@christianfocus.com**
www.christianfocus.com

The puzzles have been prepared using the New International Version of the Bible.

Cover design by Profile Design

This book and others in the series can be purchased from your local Christian bookshop. Alternatively you can write to TnT Ministries direct or place your order with the publisher.

ISBN: 1-85792-709-5

TnT Ministries (which stands for Teaching and Training Ministries) was launched in February 1993 by Christians from a broad variety of denominational backgrounds who were concerned that teaching the Bible to children be taken seriously. The leaders were in charge of the Sunday School of 50 teachers at St Helen's Bishopsgate, an evangelical church in the City of London, for 13 years, during which time a range of Biblical teaching materials was developed. TnT Ministries also runs training days for Sunday School teachers.

CONTENTS

On the Way for 11-14s / Book 6

Contributors:

Preparation of Bible material:
Wendy Barber
Thalia Blundell

Editing:
David Jackman

Activities & Puzzles:
Wendy Barber
Thalia Blundell
Rachel Garforth-Bles
Jennefer Lord
Nick Margesson
Emma Blundell

On The Way for 11-14s works on a 3 year syllabus consisting of 6 books. It builds on the 9-11s syllabus and introduces young teens to study the Bible in a way which is challenging and intellectually stretching. Because they are often unprepared to take things at face value and are encouraged to question everything, it is important to satisfy the mind while touching the heart. Therefore, some of the lessons are designed to introduce the idea of further Bible study skills, e.g. the use of a concordance, a character study, studying a single verse or a passage.

Lessons are grouped in series, each of which is introduced by a series overview stating the aims of the series, the lesson aim for each week, and an appropriate memory verse. Every lesson, in addition to an aim, has study notes to enable the teacher to understand the Bible passage, a suggestion to focus attention on the study to follow, a 'Question Section' and an activity for the group to do. The Question Section consists of 2-3 questions designed to help in discussing the application of the Bible passage. The course can be joined at any time during its 3 year cycle.

To prepare a Bible lesson properly takes at least one evening (2-3 hours). It is helpful to read the Bible passage several days before teaching it to allow time to mull over what it is saying.

When preparing a lesson the following steps should be taken -

1. PRAY!

In a busy world this is very easy to forget. We are unable to understand God's word without his help and we need to remind ourselves of that fact before we start.

2. READ THE BIBLE PASSAGE

This should be done *before* reading the lesson manual. Our resource is the Bible, not what someone says about it. The Bible study notes in the lesson manual are a commentary on the passage to help you understand it.

3. LOOK AT THE LESSON AIM

This should reflect the main teaching of the passage. Plan how that can be packaged appropriately for the age group you teach.

4. TEACHING THE BIBLE PASSAGE

This should take place in the context of simple Bible study. Do ensure that the children use the same version of the Bible. Prior to the lesson decide how the passage will be read, (e.g. one verse at a time), and who should do the reading. Is the passage short enough to read the whole of it or should some parts be paraphrased by the teacher? Work through the passage, deciding which points should be raised. Design simple questions to bring out the main teaching of the passage. The first questions should elicit the facts and should be designed so that they cannot be answered by a simple 'no' or 'yes'. If a group member reads out a Bible verse as the answer, praise him/her and then ask him/her to put it in his/her own words. Once the facts have been established go on to application questions, encouraging the group to think through how the teaching can be applied to their lives. The 'Question Section' is designed to help you when it comes to discussing the application of the Bible passage.

5. VISUAL AIDS

Pictures are very rarely required for this age group. A Bible Timeline (see previous publications for 11-14's) is useful so that the young people can see where the Bible passage they are studying comes in the big picture of God's revelation to his people. A map is helpful to demonstrate distances, etc. A flip chart or similar is handy to summarise the lesson.

6. ACTIVITIES AND PUZZLES

These are designed to reinforce the Bible teaching and very little prior preparation (if any) is required by the teacher.

- Encourages the leaders to study the Bible for themselves.

- Teaches young people Bible-study skills.

- Everything you need is in the one book, so there is no need to buy activity books.

- Undated materials allow you to use the lessons to fit your situation without wasting materials.

- Once you have the entire syllabus, there is no need to repurchase.

On The Way for 11-14s is designed to teach young teens how to read and understand a passage of Scripture and then apply it to their lives (see How to Prepare a Lesson). Before learning how to study the Bible they need to know what it is and how to find their way around it.

The Bible

Christians believe that the Bible is God's word and contains all we need to know in order to live in relationship with God and with each other. It is the way God has chosen to reveal himself to mankind; it not only records historical facts but also interprets those facts. It is not a scientific text book.

What does the Bible consist of?

The Bible is God's story. It is divided into 2 sections - the Old and New Testaments. 'Testament' means 'covenant' or 'promise'.

The Old Testament contains 39 books covering the period from creation to about 400 years before the birth of Jesus. It records God's mighty acts of creation, judgment and mercy as well as their interpretation through the words of the prophets.

The New Testament is made up of 27 books containing details of the life, death and resurrection of Jesus, the spread of the gospel in the early Church, Christian doctrine and the final judgment.

Who wrote the Bible?

The books of the Bible were written by many different people, some known and others not. Christians believe that all these authors were inspired by God (2 Peter 1:20-21, 2 Timothy 3:16). As a result we can trust what it says.

THE BIBLE LIBRARY

To make a chart of the Bible Library enlarge the template below and photocopy as required. Draw 2 sets of shelves on a large piece of paper (see diagram). Label the shelves. Cut off the unwanted books from each set and write the names of the books on the spines. Glue the books onto the appropriate shelves in the order in which they appear in the Bible.

How can we find our way around it?

Each book in the Bible is divided into chapters, each one of which contains a number of verses. When the Books were written originally the chapter and verse divisions were absent. These have been added to enable the readers to find their way around. When written down they are recorded in the following way, Genesis 5:1-10. This tells us to look up the book of Genesis, chapter 5, verses 1 to 10.

At the front of the Bible is a contents page, listing the books in the order in which they come in the Bible. It is perfectly acceptable to look up the index to see which page to turn to.

Aids to teach the Bible passage

*   Many of the lessons have activity pages that help to bring out the main teaching of the Bible passage.
*   Packs of maps and charts can be purchased from Christian book shops.
*   A Bible Time Line is useful to reinforce the chronology of the Bible (see other titles in this series).

Questions to aid in understanding

Periodically use the following questions to help the young people understand the passage:

*   Who wrote it?
*   To whom was it written?
*   When was it written?
*   What situation is being described? (if applicable)

The Bible Library

Old Testament	New Testament
Law (5 books)	Gospels & Acts (5)
History (12 books)	Paul's Epistles (13)
Poetry & Wisdom (5)	Other Epistles (8)
Prophets (17 books)	Prophecy (1 book)

OVERVIEW
Psalms

Week 1   **God is My Refuge**   *Psalm 16:1-11*
To teach that God is the only source of true security, both in this present life and in the future.

Week 2   **God is My Judge**   *Psalm 73:1-28*
To understand that those who do wrong will be judged, even though they appear to be successful in this life.

Week 3   **God is My Maker**   *Psalm 90:1-17*
To teach that without God we are nothing.

Week 4   **God is My Protector**   *Psalm 121:1-8*
To teach that God is able to protect us at all times and in every situation.

Week 5   **God is My King**   *Psalm 145:1-21*
To understand why God is worthy of praise.

SERIES AIMS

1. To get a more rounded view of God's character.

2. To learn a proper reverence for God in the light of the above.

MEMORY WORK

Great is the Lord and most worthy of praise; his greatness no-one can fathom.

Psalm 145:3

6

A Selection of Psalms

The Psalter was the hymn book used in Temple worship following the return from exile. However, the psalms are not merely hymns but are also a means of teaching, e.g. Psalm 34 where each verse begins with a letter of the Hebrew alphabet, and call for a personal response from the hearer. All psalms are addressed to God or speak about him. They speak about the God of Israel, who brought his people out of Egypt, made a covenant with them, and who cares for and defends his people. No psalm asks for eternal salvation, although some cry for forgiveness (Psalm 51) and some speak of a future hope. The Old Testament Jew had no developed theology of a final judgement and many of the psalms cry out to God for judgement on the wicked here and now (Psalms 35, 69). The Psalms are written from the standpoint of God's people, who had a special relationship with him. The Psalter is split into 5 books and these were used in public worship in conjunction with the 5 books of the Torah (Genesis - Deuteronomy).

Book	Psalms	Torah	General Comment
I	1-41	Genesis	creation, sin and redemption
II	42-72	Exodus	the nation of Israel - ruined and redeemed
III	73-89	Leviticus	God's holiness, the temple, God on the throne
IV	90-106	Numbers	the relationship of Israel and God's Kingdom with surrounding nations
V	107-150	Deuteronomy	God and his word, praise hymns

Each of the 5 sections ends with a doxology.

The Psalter was completed and put in order during the time of Ezra, although many of the psalms date from an earlier period, e.g. Psalm 90 (a prayer of Moses), psalms written by David. Almost half the psalms are attributed to David. Many of these are thought to have been written by him, although "of David" can also mean "in the manner of/authorised by David". Other authors are Solomon (2), Asaph and the Sons of Korah (24), Heman (1), Ethan (1) and Moses (1) leaving 48 unaccounted for. Asaph and the Sons of Korah were groups of temple administrators from the time of Solomon who were responsible for temple worship. Some psalms, e.g. 137, were written during the time of Ezra and the rebuilding of the second temple.

Some of the psalms were used on specific occasions, e.g.

Psalm 81	Feast of Tabernacles
Psalms 113-118	Passover
Psalms 120-134	Sung by pilgrims on their way to Jerusalem to celebrate the 3 annual festivals
Psalm 130	The Day of Atonement

When reading the psalms the following points are useful:

1. They were written to Jews. How do today's Jews interpret them, and why do Christians interpret them differently? e.g. Psalm 22. This psalm was written by David and gives useful insight into his situation, but the Jew sees no reference to the Messiah. For the Jew, the Messiah is not meant to suffer but will come in glory to reign. The psalms also give the modern Jew help in knowing how to praise and pray to God.

2. Jesus and Peter quoted from them in order to prove the point being made.

    e.g.   Matthew 21:16   cf. Psalm 8:2
           Matthew 21:42   cf. Psalm 118:22-23
           Acts 2:25-28   cf. Psalm 16:8-11
           Acts 2:34-35   cf. Psalm 110:1

    This demonstrates that Jesus and the early church found the psalms authoritative and useful.

3. The following psalms contain references to the Messiah:

The anointed King	Psalm 2:1-2	cf. Acts 4:25-26
	Psalm 45:6-7	cf. Hebrews 1:9
	Psalm 110:1	cf. Luke 20:41-44, Hebrews 1:13
God's Son	Psalm 2:7	cf. Hebrews 1:5
God	Psalm 45: 6-7	cf. Hebrews 1:9
	Psalm 68:18	cf. Ephesians 4:7-8
	Psalm 102:25-27	cf. Hebrews 1:10-12
Suffering servant	Psalm 22:1	cf. Matthew 27:50
	Psalm 35:19	cf. John 15:25
	Psalm 40: 6-8	cf. Hebrews 10:5-7
	Psalm 41:9	cf. John 13:18
	Psalm 69:9	cf. John 2:17
	Psalm 118:22-23	cf. Matthew 21:42-44, Acts 4:11
	Psalm 118:26	cf. Matthew 23:39

This series looks at 5 psalms, 1 from Book I (Psalm 16), 1 from Book III (Psalm 73), 1 from Book IV (Psalm 90) and 2 from Book V (Psalms 121 and 145). All of them give insights into the character of God and his relationship with his people.

PREPARATION
Psalm 16:1-11

LESSON AIMS

To teach that God is the only source of true security, both in this life and the future.

This psalm was written by David, but his circumstances at the time are not known.

16:1   A refuge is a place of shelter from danger, trouble, etc.

16:2   God is the only source of well being (cf. Ps 73:25).

16:3   In the Septuagent, the Greek word chosen to translate the Hebrew word 'saints' is the same as the New Testament word, where it speaks of all Christians. In the Old Testament it is usually applied to heavenly beings, but the addition of 'in the land' makes it clear that here it should be taken in its NT sense. David finds his friends from among God's people.

16:4   This verse speaks of the situation of those who follow other gods. Libations of blood were the sacrifices poured out on the altars of counterfeit gods. By not taking up their names David is saying he would not appeal to them or worship them.

16:5-6   The portion or inheritance refers to what the Lord had given his people both in terms of land and of himself. When the Israelites came back to Canaan from Egypt the land was portioned out by Joshua, Eliezer the priest and the tribal heads (Joshua 14:1-5). This was done by dividing the land up into sections and then each section was allocated by casting lots. A 'lot' was a two sided disc believed to be under the control of God when thrown. The results of the throw were used to determine God's will (Proverbs 16:33). Once allocated, the bounderies of the piece of land were marked out, and to alter them was to alter God's gift (Deuteronomy 19:14). Numbers 18:20 speaks of God himself being the inheritance of the priests who had no land to call their own. In the same way God is David's heritage.

16:7   God counsels rather than coerces. Night time is when troubles loom large and keep people awake. There is no note of anxiety in this verse, rather a calm confidence that God will bring David to the right decision.

16:8   See Psalm 73:23. God is at David's right hand in the sense of standing beside him to help, perhaps in a court or in a battle.

16:8-11   See Acts 2:25-32.

QUESTIONS

1.   What would you expect to inherit from your parents when they die? What entitles a person to their inheritance? So, according to this psalm, what is our inheritance and what entitles us to get it?

2   What help does this psalm give for those times when we are troubled?

Home Base Divide the group into 2 teams. Give each member of one team a piece of red wool and each member of the opposing team a piece of blue wool. The piece of wool represents the team member's 'life'.

The aim of the game is for members to collect the opposite team's pieces of wool and return to their home base without losing their own lives. Wool is obtained from an opposing team member by placing both hands on their shoulders to tag them. Once a team member has been tagged he/she must return to their home base to pick up another piece of wool. No one can be tagged when they are at their home base. Leaders can run around during the game to provide further danger and obstacles to avoid. After a set period of time has elapsed, call the game to a halt and count up the number of pieces of wool collected. The winning team is the one that has collected the most.

Link into the Bible study by pointing out things may be tough, like in the game, but being with God is like being at our home base. God is the only place where we find true security for both this life and the next.

ACTIVITY

Photocopy page 11 for each group member.

There are no clues to this puzzle. First crack the code with the help of the given letters. When you have finished, the shaded words will complete the Bible verse at the foot of the page.

The grid contains given letters: **I** (at 3), **SAFE** (at 7, 9, 8, 26).

Code key:

1	2	3	4	5	6	7	8	9	10	11	12	13
		I				S	F	A				

14	15	16	17	18	19	20	21	22	23	24	25	26

Great is the .... and most .... of .... ;

his .... no-one can ....

From which verse in Psalm 145 does this come?

PREPARATION
Psalm 73:1-28

LESSON AIMS

To understand that those who do wrong will be judged, even though they appear successful in this life.

This is a psalm which addresses one of the problems experienced by the prophets in the OT, namely how is it the wicked seem to prosper and the godly suffer? We see this demonstrated in full in the Book of Job. The structure of the psalm consists of two halves each made up of 13 verses, framed by v.1 and v.27. The 2 halves are in marked contrast to each other. Psalm 73 is a psalm of Asaph, who was the leader of one of David's Levitical choirs. This psalm begins a collection of 11 psalms of Asaph, which are dominated by the theme of God's rule over his people and the nations.

73:1	'Pure in heart' is to do with right attitudes and motives. 'Pure' means being totally committed to God. The 'heart' is the centre of the human spirit from which comes thoughts, feelings, motivations and actions. This verse makes a statement about God's goodness to his people, in spite of the evidence to the contrary (v.3-12).
73:2	This verse speaks of a crisis of faith.
73:3	The reason for the slip was envy and looking away from God.
73:4	Health and strength is still viewed in some Christian circles as a believer's right, despite this passage and NT passages such as Romans 8:18-23.
73:6-9	These verses list the characteristics of the ungodly.
73:9	The ungodly admit to no one's right of jurisdiction over them. They are their own kings.
73:10	This verse speaks of the popular worship of success.
73:11	The psalmist here is talking about God receiving little or no respect and sin being well thought of.

73:13-14	The psalmist contrasts his lot with that of the ungodly, concluding that he has wasted his time in seeking to live a holy life.
73:15	The tenor of the psalm changes at this point when the psalmist realises that what he is saying is betrayal of God's people.
73:16-17	The psalmist stops feeling sorry for himself (see v.3,13) and turns to God for help.
73:17	The light dawns. He centres his attention on God and everything falls into place.
73:18-20	Though the wicked seem to prosper God has allowed their position to become precarious. Their final destiny will be separation from God.
73:21-22	The psalmist sees himself as he was in his earlier state (v.2-3) and repents. When he was taken up with grief and bitterness he was like an animal with no understanding.
73:23-26	The psalmist recognises that the reality of his relationship with God is all to do with who God is, and nothing to do with his circumstances.
73:23-24	God's counsel has overcome his foolishness and God will guide him to the end of his days (see Psalm 16:7-8).
73:25	Though at the beginning of the psalm he envied the prosperity of the wicked, now he realises that nothing else is more desirable than God.
73:26	'My flesh and my heart may fail' means death.
	Since the psalmist was a Levite the Lord was his portion in the promised

land (Numbers 18:20). Here he confesses that God himself is his preserver, sustainer and his very life.

73:28   This verse explains why the psalmist can write verse 1.

1. Envy is something that destroys our relationship with God and with other people. Can you think of any characters in the Bible who allowed envy to spoil their relationship with each other?

2. What lesson can you learn from this psalm about the right and wrong ways to deal with envy?

Stars in Their Eyes   Before the session, cut out pictures of 'successful' people from magazines and newspapers. Choose people from a variety of professions, such as actors, models, singers, sports stars, academics, TV presenters, etc. Glue the pictures onto separate pieces of card, disguising their faces in some way, e.g. covering up the eyes, adding a hat, adding a moustache, etc. Number each card on the front.

Stick the cards up around the room. Give each group member a pen and piece of paper and ask them to identify each celebrity and what makes them famous. The winner is the person to get most right. You might want to play a song with apt lyrics as background music whilst the above is happening.
Point out that we do not know whether or not these celebrities are Christian, but many people who appear successful and fulfilled are turning their backs on God. Let's see what the Bible says will happen to them.

Photocopy page 14 for each group member.

In the word square you will find the following 16 words describing the evildoer. Each word reads in a straight line horizontally, vertically or diagonally and can read forwards or backwards. No letter is used more than once.

ARROGANT	HEALTHY	PROUD	VIOLENT
CALLOUS	MALICIOUS	SCOFFER	WEALTHY
CAREFREE	OPPRESSOR	STRONG	WICKED
CONCEITED	PROSPEROUS	THREATENING	WRONGDOER

G	T	H	R	E	A	T	E	N	I	N	G	O
S	U	O	L	L	A	C	D	S	I	O	S	T
P	H	E	S	W	T	R	C	E	P	N	C	G
R	R	T	M	H	E	O	O	P	F	M	A	Y
O	D	E	H	A	F	A	R	E	A	R	R	D
S	E	T	O	F	L	E	L	T	A	Y	E	E
P	K	S	E	D	S	I	N	T	H	N	F	T
E	C	R	T	S	G	A	C	T	H	P	R	I
R	I	D	O	R	G	N	L	I	R	Y	E	E
O	W	R	M	O	O	A	O	O	O	Y	E	C
U	P	O	R	R	E	N	U	R	T	U	I	N
S	O	R	N	H	F	D	G	O	W	R	S	O
E	A	V	E	T	N	E	L	O	I	V	R	C

Now, starting from the top and reading from left to right, write down the remaining letters to discover what enables the Christian to keep going in difficult circumstances.

From which verse does this come?

PREPARATION
Psalm 90:1-17

LESSON AIMS
To teach that without God we are nothing.

This psalm was written by Moses. In it there are 2 sections which describe the human condition under God's righteous anger (vv.3-6,7-10). These are framed by two couplets which speak of God's power and his relationship with his people (vv.1-2,11-12). The psalm ends with the concluding prayer of v.13-17.

90:1   Note the use of Lord to describe God. This is not God's covenant name, LORD, so is referring to God as master.

        Dwelling place (or refuge) is a similar metaphor to the one used by Moses in Deuteronomy 33:27.

90:2   A reminder of the sovereignty and permanence of God. This is a contrast to man's short life span (v.3-6).

90:4   Dust alludes to the curse of Adam (Genesis 3:19).

        For God 1,000 years are like a short watch in the night. In other words, time as man sees it is meaningless set against God's time scale of eternity.

90:7-10   Man's troubles. The short life of man is filled with trouble, as God searches out and knows our every sin and makes us feel his righteous anger.

90:11-12   No one can properly imagine God's wrath, but we can all take stock of the brevity of our lives and our accountability to God. Moses asks God for wisdom in the way he lives his life. Here is a warning not to put things off to a later date.

90:13   Moses asks God to relent, or turn back, and have mercy, in contrast to v.3 where men were turned to dust.

90:14-15   Contrast these verses with v.9. Moses' prayer for God's compassion was finally answered in the death and resurrection of Jesus (Romans 5:2-5; 8:18, 2 Corinthians 14:17).

90:16-17   The contrast continues here between what was seen as perishable in verses 3-12 and the eternal glory of God's deeds.

QUESTIONS

1. In this psalm we see the insignificance of our life span in the light of eternity (v.3-6). What does this teach us about the way we should live?

2. What does this psalm teach about sin?

3. What comfort is there for us in this psalm?

FOCUS ACTIVITY

Essential Air. Get the members of the group to hold their breath for as long as possible. Award a small prize to the person who holds their breath for the longest. Point out that everyone had to breathe eventually, even the person who held their breath for the longest. Air is essential for our survival - without air we are nothing. The same is true with God - without him we are nothing.

ACTIVITY

Photocopy page 16 for each group member. The remaining word is 'compassion' from verse 13.

All the following words from Psalm 90 can be found in letter pairs in the grid. The words read either horizontally, vertically or diagonally and can read backwards or forwards, but the letter pairs will always read from left to right. No letter pair is used more than once. One word on the list has been done to show you. When you have found all the listed words you will be left with a word that tells us what Moses asked God to do.

ARIGHT	FEAR	PASS	SINS
CHILDREN	GLAD	PRESENCE	SORROW
CONSUMED	INIQUITIES	RELENT	STRENGTH
DAYS	LENGTH	REST	THOUSAND
DUST	LORD	RETURN	WISDOM
EIGHTY	LOVE	SECRET	WITHERED
FAVOUR	NUMBER	SERVANTS	WORK

ER	ES	TI	UI	IQ	IN	ON	TH
EN	MB	LE	NG	TH	SI	WI	NG
DR	PA	NU	NT	AS	AD	SD	RE
IL	SS	DA	MP	LE	GL	OM	ST
CH	FA	CO	YS	WI	RE	FE	SE
RK	WO	VO	TH	RN	AR	CR	ED
TH	SE	ER	UR	TU	ET	UM	HT
OU	ED	RV	PR	RE	NS	IG	SO
SA	TY	ES	AN	CO	AR	RR	LO
ND	EN	GH	VE	TS	OW	RD	DU
CE	RE	ST	EI	LO	NS	SI	ST

What is the remaining word and which verse is it from?

PREPARATION
Psalm 121:1-8

LESSON AIMS
To teach that God is able to protect us at all times and in every situation.

This psalm was one of the group (Psalms 120 - 134) sung by pilgrims as they journeyed from their homes to Jerusalem for one or more of the great festivals of the year. Believing Jews were expected to travel to the Temple at Jerusalem to celebrate the 3 great feasts of Passover, Weeks (Pentecost) and Tabernacles. Psalm 121 is the middle one of the three dealing with the journey from home to Jerusalem. Psalm 120 speaks of the home situation (Psalm 120:5) and Psalm 122 of arrival at Jerusalem. Psalm 121 speaks of the need for protection on the journey.

This psalm is composed of 4 couplets, each having an introductory line from which the rest of the couplet develops.

121:1   The reference to hills could mean different things. The hills could be a place of safety, (cf. Psalm 11:1), or a place of danger, e.g. the haunt of robbers. Another suggestion is that it refers to the sight of Jerusalem set on the hill of Mount Zion.

121:2   Whatever the explanation of the question in v.1, this verse supplies the answer. The Maker of the universe is the pilgrims' helper.

121:3   The word used for 'not' in this verse implies a request. God is being asked to look after the pilgrim when the way is treacherous. (In this psalm, from v.3 onwards, the word used for 'you' is singular.) It is worth remembering that the pilgrims walked with bare or sandalled feet, often for long and weary days in the hot sun (v.5).

God is not like Baal, he does not slumber (see 1 Kings 18:27)!

121:4   This verse answers the question of v.3. The Lord of all creation is the one on whom his people can lean, in whom they can trust.

121:5   Shade was important on a hot journey.

'Right hand' - see Psalm 16:8.

121:6   The sun and moon encompass all the troubles which could attack or threaten them during the day or the night.

121:7   Keep you from all harm does not imply an easy life, but a well armed one, cf. Psalm 23:4. A dark valley can be faced with God's help.

121:8   Your coming and going is a literary device called inclusion. It encompasses everything in between the two extremes, i.e. in this case the whole of life.

QUESTIONS

1. Split this psalm into its 4 couplets and give each one a title.

2. In what ways is life a pilgrimage? Go through the psalm verse by verse and list all the benefits that God promises the pilgrim.

Protection Racket. Choose one member of the group to hold onto an item, such as a tennis ball or flag. The other group members have to get the item off the person, but the leaders (or one particularly large leader) act as protectors.

Obviously, care must be taken with physical contact games to prevent people being hurt, so the leaders will need to make sure that the situation does not get out of control. Allow a set period of time for the game, then bring it to a halt.

In this game it does not really matter whether or not the leaders are able to protect the person holding the item. If it does work, link into the Bible study by pointing out that, just as the leaders protected thd person, God is able to protect us. If it does not work point out that God's protection is so much better!

ACTIVITY

Photocopy page 19 for each group member.

In this puzzle the answers to the clues are entered in the grid in a clockwise direction around the spiral. Each answer starts from its clue number and the last letter of one answer is the first letter of the next one. The answers can be found in today's Bible passage.

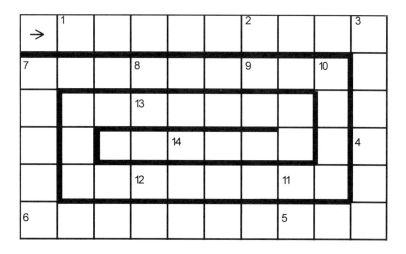

1. God's people.
2. God will watch over your ....
3. What I lift up.
4. What is at your right hand?
5. God watches over you now and ....
6. God made this.
7. The sun will not do this.
8. The light in the night sky.
9. The present.
10. God does this over Israel.
11. I lift my eyes to these.
12. God never does this.
13. God is your shade here (2 words).
14. The opposite of night.

PREPARATION

Psalm 145:1-21

LESSON AIMS

To understand why God is worthy of praise.

This is an acrostic psalm in which each verse is introduced by a different letter of the Hebrew alphabet. In the standard Hebrew text one letter of the alphabet is lacking, but in most ancient versions the missing letter is supplied in the couplet at the end of v.13. Some commentators question the addition of the verse, making the point that Hebrew poetry subordinates form to meaning and it may have been the poet's intention to omit one letter to indicate that no human mind can fully grasp the glories of God, even with the help of revelation (see the IVP New Bible Commentary 21st Century Edition, p.581).

The psalm consists of an introduction (v.1-2) and conclusion (v.21) with four poetic paragraphs in between, each introduced by a thematic line (vv.3,8,13b,17).

145:1-2	God is king and is worthy of praise every day and for ever.
145:3-7	God's mighty acts are displayed, showing his greatness (v.3) and his goodness (v.7).
145:8-9	God's compassion makes him worthy of praise. Cf. Exodus 34:6-7 where God reveals himself to his covenant people. Verse 9 broadens out the extent of God's goodness.
145:10-13a	The splendours of God's kingdom make him worthy of praise. The saints (those who are set apart for God's purpose) will do the following, extol God (v.10), tell of his glory (v.11) and speak of his might (v.11) for the express purpose of making known God's goodness and greatness.
145:13b-16	God's faithfulness makes him worthy of praise. He can be trusted to keep his promises.
145:13b	Faithful and loving are also combined in Psalm 36:5.

145:14	God helps the inadequate, i.e. everybody.
145:15-16	These verses reflect the generosity of God's provision.
145:17-20	God's righteousness makes him worthy of praise.
145:18	God is near, (the next-of-kin), to his people who pray to him, but he requires sincerity (v.18), reverence (v.19), and their love (v.20).

QUESTIONS

1. This psalm focuses on the character of God and what he has done. How can this focus help us when we pray?

2. List all the characteristics of God mentioned in this psalm. How do we know that this is a true picture of God? (What passages of the Bible demonstrate these truths?)

Praise Brainstorm. On a large sheet of paper ask the group to list all of the things that they can think of to praise God for. Make it clear that they can be large things or small and that you are not looking for 'correct' answers, but rather that you want as large a list as possible.

Let's see what the Bible has to say about praising God and how many of these things are mentioned in Psalm 145.

Finish the Bible study with a time of prayer, praising God (see below).

Divide the group into twos or threes and ask them to write an alphabet with each letter describing a characteristic of God.

Praying with young teens

We need to encourage the young people to pray out loud.

Discuss with the group what they have learnt from the passage and ask for any prayer requests.

Go round the group in order, asking each member what they will pray about. It is important for the young people to know what they are praying about and in which order.

Encourage the entire group to be involved, but never force them to pray.

Suggest they restrict their prayers to one or two sentences, as this is manageable. It can be very off-putting for those who are learning to pray if one of the group prays beautifully for 5 minutes!

OVERVIEW
The Normal
Christian Life

Week 6 | **Bible Reading**
To understand why we need to read the Bible and the importance of doing it regularly.

Week 7 | **Prayer**
To understand the importance of prayer and why it is an essential part of our relationship with God.

Week 8 | **Obedience and Discipline**
To understand why God requires our obedience and the need to be disciplined in our relationship with him.

Week 9 | **Witness**
To understand why we should tell others about Jesus and how to do it.

Week 10 | **Fellowship**
To understand the importance of meeting with other Christians if we are to persevere in the Christian life.

Week 11 | **Service**
To understand why God calls us to serve one another and to work out how we can do it in our situations.

Week 12 | **The Holy Spirit**
To understand the work of the indwelling Holy Spirit in progressive sanctification.

SERIES AIMS

1. To learn about the componants that make up a normal Christian life and that they are not optional.

2. To encourage one another to put them into practice.

MEMORY WORK

Therefore, I urge you, brothers, in view of God's mercy, to offer your bodies as living sacrifices, holy and pleasing to God - this is your spiritual act of worship. Do not conform any longer to the pattern of this world, but be transformed by the renewing of your mind. Then you will be able to test and approve what God's will is - his good, pleasing and perfect will.

Romans 12:1-2

The Normal Christian Life

Children growing up in Christian homes often take the Bible, prayer, etc. for granted. Young teenagers are at a stage in their lives when they are beginning to question their parents' attitudes on all manner of things, so this is a good opportunity to look at the things we do as Christians and discover whether they are essential for Christian maturity or just optional. This series aims to introduce the components that should be part of a normal Christian life and allow the teens to take their spiritual temperature.

The first three sessions look at the individual's relationship with God, the first one being on the Bible and the importance of reading it regularly. Young people who have grown up in Christian homes may well not read the Bible on their own, relying on family Bible readings. Often boys find reading on their own more difficult than girls. It is important not to assume anything, but to find out what is happening in your group. We need to inculcate helpful habits into our young people, because these will stand them in good stead when they leave us to go on to further education or employment. The second session looks at prayer and why it is an essential componant of our relationship with God and this is followed by a lesson on obedience and discipline. Learning about God from his word is no good unless we put what we learn into practice.

The next three lessons look at our relationship with each other and cover witnessing, fellowship and service. Quite often our young people have a desire to tell their friends about Jesus, but do not know how to do it, so the session on witnessing teaches them how to present the gospel simply and accurately. This is followed by a lesson looking at fellowship and the importance of meeting together regularly to encourage each other in living as Christians. The sixth session is about service and looks at how our young people can be involved in serving in their local churches.

The series ends with a study on progressive sanctification, looking at the way the indwelling Holy Spirit energises us to put all these things into practice. Our sinful nature encourages us towards legalism and dependence on our own efforts, so we must ensure that our young people realise their need to be changed from the inside, rather than assuming that the Christian life is about adding in a series of externals.

PREPARATION
See Lesson Notes

LESSON AIMS
To understand why we need to read the Bible and the importance of doing it regularly.

Introduction
Use the focus activity at the start of the session. Ask the group members to say what the Bible is and why we should read and study it. Record their answers on a board or flipchart.

Why should we read the Bible?

Hebrews 4:12-13
These verses come at the end of a section commenting on Psalm 95 (3:1 - 4:11). The author of Hebrews warns his readers to listen to God's voice, so that they will not become hardened by sin and turn their backs on God.

4:12   God's word is living and active, which implies that it has an effect on those who hear it and it achieves its end. This does not mean that everyone who hears it will respond positively (see 4:6).
        The 'heart' is the control centre of the person and involves mind and will. Note that God's word penetrates to the very centre of our being and judges our thoughts and attitudes.

4:13   We may be able to hide our thoughts and attitudes from other people, but not from God.

If God knows us in this way, then what he has to say is vitally important. God's word applies just as much to our generation and culture as it did to the people to whom it was originally written, because his character does not change and he always does what he says he will do.

2 Timothy 3:14-17

3:15   The Scriptures teach us how we can be saved. (NB in Paul's day this was mainly the Old Testament.)

3:16   All Scripture is inspired by God. This tells us the origin of the Scriptures and, therefore, why they are profitable.
        Teaching and rebuking - God's word teaches doctrine and rebukes error.

Correcting and training in righteousness are to do with behaviour. We must not divorce what we do from what we believe, which is a prevalent attitude in post-modern society.

3:17   The result is that God's servants are equipped for every good work. Everything we need to know in order to have a right relationship with God and with other people is found in Scripture. There are no new doctrines.

When should we read it?
Can you get to know someone if you never spend time with them, listening to what they say about themselves and about their views on what is happening in the world?

Psalm 1:1-6
This psalm describes two categories of men - the righteous and the wicked. The righteous man is the one who delights in God's law and meditates on it day and night (v.2).

Deuteronomy 6:4-9
These verses are part of Moses' instructions to God's people as they were about to enter the promised Land.

6:7   The people were to talk to each other (and to their children!) about God's word. At home, walking along the road, when you go to bed and when you get up. There is not a lot of time left. God's word should impinge on every aspect of our lives and should come into conversations quite naturally as we go about our daily lives. The Bible is not just for church and Sunday.

How should we read it?
Is it enough to read it as an academic exercise, or should it be put into practice?

James 1:22-25

1:22   It is possible to listen to God's word regularly, but never to let it affect our lives.

If we do this we deceive ourselves about our standing with God.

1:23-24   If we do not act on what we hear we soon forget what we have learned.

1:25   God's word brings freedom. It is worth pointing this out to the young people. So often they think of God's word as a straitjacket, preventing their enjoyment of life. The result of putting God's word into practice is blessing.

What should my attitude be to the Bible?

Psalm 19:7-11

19:7   'Law' is a comprehensive term for God's revealed will.
'perfect' - see Romans 12:2.
'revive' is to give new life to.
'statutes/testimony' - truth attested by God (1 John 5:9).
'trustworthy/sure' - firm, confirmed.

19:8   'precepts and commands' - God is specific about what he requires from us and his words are authoritative.
'right' - morally right/straight.

19:9   'fear' - the response brought about by hearing God's word.
'pure' - see Psalm 12:6.
'ordinances/judgments' - judicial decisions God has made known regarding various human predicaments.
'sure/true' - dependable.
'altogether' - all alike, i.e. everyone of them.

19:11   The purpose of God's word is to cause a response in the hearer and a subsequent change of direction. The hearer is warned to turn from his own way and follow God by keeping his commands.

Implications

1. The Bible is God's living word and contains everything we need in order to live in right relationship with God and with each other.
2. If we truly believe this, we are foolish if we do not read it.
3. It is not enough to read God's word as an academic exercise; we must put it into practice.

Application

We need to spend some time discussing the following:

1. What stops us reading the Bible regularly?
   - lack of time
   - lack of a suitable place
   - more important things to do
   - too tired
   - don't know how or where to start

2. Does it matter if we do not read the Bible on our own as long as we read it with our families?

3. What things can help us to read the Bible on our own?
   - Bible reading notes - have some to show
   - Encouragement from each other

It would be helpful to encourage the young people to make a contract to try and read the Bible for 10 minutes every day for the next week. This may seem tough, but it is much easier to remember to do it daily, than for 3 or 4 days in the week.

Get the group members to make a list of how they spend their time in a typical day - at school, travelling, doing homework, talking on the telephone, watching television, with friends, sleeping. Discuss where they could find 10 minutes to spend reading the Bible. Provide each person with a list of short passages, one per day, for the following week.

Play charades, using titles of films, TV series or books. Choose titles that they should know and play 3-5 games, depending on the time. For a large group it is preferable to divide into teams, with team members taking it in turns to act out the title to their teams. Finish with 'The Bible'.

This week we are learning about the place of the Bible in the normal Christian life.

PREPARATION

See Lesson Notes

LESSON AIMS

To understand the importance of prayer and why it's essential to our relationship with God.

Introduction

1. Discuss how the group has gone with their Bible reading during the past week. Encourage them to keep going.

2. The Focus activity.

3. Ask the group to define 'prayer'.

Prayer, at its simplest, is a conversation with God. God opens the conversation (the Bible) and we respond (prayer). It is important for the young people to realise that prayer is not something we do naturally, but is a response to God. Christian prayer can only occur if God has touched that person's spirit. God does not, therefore, guarantee to hear every person's prayer (Isaiah 1:15; 29:13). True prayer involves the recognition and acceptance of God's will in that situation, and is based on God's mercy and willingness to forgive rather than on our own good deeds.

John Bunyan defines prayer as 'a sincere, sensible, affectionate pouring out of the heart or soul to God through Christ, in the strength and assistance of the Holy Spirit, for such things as God hath promised, or, according to the Word, for the good of the Church, with submission, in Faith, to the Will of God.' (John Bunyan, *The Doctrine of the Law and Grace unfolded* and *I will pray with the Spirit*, ed. Richard L. Greaves (1976) p.235)

How should we pray?

Prayer is hard work (Paul records Epaphras as 'wrestling in prayer' in Colossians 4:12). We need to remind the young people of this so that they do not get discouraged or think something is wrong when prayer does not come easily.

The following formula can be helpful: ACTS - Adoration, Confession, Thanksgiving, Supplication.

Nehemiah

1:5   Adoration. 'Great and awesome God' demonstrates his reverential approach to God. By using the term 'covenant of love' Nehemiah is showing his confidence in God's love.

1:6-7   Confession. A true sense of God's greatness results in an awareness of the depths of our own sinfulness. Nehemiah confesses his own sin and that of his family and the people of Israel.

1:8-11   Supplication. Nehemiah takes seriously what God has already said in his word (Deuteronomy 30:1-5)and calls upon him to do it. His prayer was based on Scripture.

Nehemiah prayed for the success of his plan (v.11).

Luke

11:1-4   We need to put God's concerns before our own - God's name, God's kingdom and God's will come before my need for bread, forgiveness and victory.

Matthew

6:5-7   They are told how not to pray. Prayer should not have the aim of impressing others (as do the hypocrites), nor trying to impress God (through endless words). Rather, prayer should express the relationship we have with a heavenly Father, who is aware of our needs (v.8) and will answer our prayers (v.6).

Luke

18:1-8   God and the Judge are contrasted not compared, e.g. the contrast between 'for a while he refused' (the judge) and 'will he delay' (of God). If even an unjust judge will grant justice to those who ask, how much more can we trust in the certainty and swiftness of God's answer.

A sign of true discipleship is the practice of constant contact with God, who the Christian knows will always hear his prayer. The answer will not always be what he hopes for; sometimes it is 'no', often 'wait'. He learns that God answers speedily when he prays, so encouraging him to pray more often. In this way the

Christian learns the importance of persisting in prayer.

When should we pray?

Prayer should go hand in hand with Bible reading, so there will be set times of day when we come to God in prayer. However, we must encourage the young people to take things to God throughout the day, not just at bedtime or when they get up.

Psalm 55:16-17 records David crying to the Lord in distress.

1 Thessalonians 5:16-18 talks about praying continually. We should take everything to God in prayer, the good things as well as the bad. Saying thank you to God when good things happen is a helpful habit to form.

What should we pray about?

Philippians

4:6-7	We should take all our anxieties to God. A lot of time is wasted by worrying about things unnecessarily. Note the injunction to present our requests **with thanksgiving**. When we take our worries to God his peace acts as a sentry to our hearts.

1 Timothy

2:1-4	We should pray for other people, not just for ourselves, and especially for those in authority over us. Note the reason - that we may live quiet lives, able to worship God freely and to proclaim the gospel, so that people will be saved.

Matthew 21:21-22, John 15:7

At first sight these verses seem to imply that if we have enough faith God will give us whatever we ask for. The prayer of faith is prayer offered to a sovereign God, confident of his willingness to do what is best for the person prayed for (cf. Luke 11:5-13). It is not stating that, if we can work up enough faith to believe without doubting, God will give us whatever we ask for. We cannot, and must not, try to manipulate God. In John 15:7 the point is made that the branch is in close relationship with the vine. A Christian, who is in close relationship with Jesus, will pray that God's will be done in all things.

Does God always answer?

'Unanswered' prayer can be a real problem for young people. They live in a culture, which expects to have things 'now' and finds the concept of waiting for something unacceptable. Thus, they expect their prayers to be answered immediately and in the affirmative. We need to remind them that, although God sometimes graciously answers the desperate cry for help from the unbeliever, the only guaranteed way into his presence is through the blood of Jesus (Romans 5:1-2). It is God's Holy Spirit living within us who enables us to pray (Romans

8:15). Only the Christian can **expect** God to answer his or her prayers (Isaiah 59:1-2).

1 John

5:14-15	God will hear us if we pray in accordance with his will.

Psalms

66:16-20	God will not hear us if we are cherishing sin in our hearts. When we come to God for help it should be with praise and thanksgiving and with sincerity.

James

4:2-3	Both lifestyle and motives are important. God will not answer selfish prayers.

Suggested approach

1. Introduction as above.

2. Divide the group into twos and threes and ask each small group to look up one of the Bible references, find out what it says about prayer and report back to the rest of the group. Go through the session raising each point and asking for feedback from the appropriate group. Record the answers on a flipchart, so that everyone in the group can keep up with what is being discovered.

3. Look at the following examples of intercessory prayer and discuss why God answered one in the affirmative, but not the other. Genesis 20:17-18, Exodus 32:30-35

4. Finish with a time of prayer (see Praying with Young Teens on page 21).

Divide the group into pairs and ask them to devise a conversation between 2 given people to act out to the group, so that the group can identify the people concerned. Suggested pairs are: doctor/patient, boyfriend/girlfriend, teacher/pupil, parent/child, boss/someone being interviewed for a job, football manager/footballer.

This week we will learn about conversations between God and us and why they are important in the normal Christian life.

PREPARATION
See Lesson Notes

LESSON AIMS
Why God requires obedience and the need to be disciplined in our relationship with him

Introduction

1. Use the focus activity to introduce the concept of obedience.

   Define obedience. Dictionary definition: submission to authority, compliance with the will of the speaker.

2. Discuss rules - why do we need them?
   - what happens when they are absent?
   - are there good and bad rules?
   - how do you decide whether a rule is good or bad?
   - who should make the rules?

3. Link to the Bible study by reminding the group of one of the things learned in Week 6, reading the Bible is no good if you do not put it into practice (James 1:22-25).

   Let's see what the Bible has to say about obedience.

Why should we be obedient?

Ecclesiastes 12:13-14

Ecclesiastes is a collection of royal teachings in the tradition of Solomon. These verses come at the end of the book.

12:13   Part of our duty to God is to keep his commands.

12:14   God will be our judge and he knows our inmost thoughts.

John 14:21-24

These verses form part of Jesus' teaching just before his arrest and crucifixion.

14:21   Obeying Jesus' commands (words) is inextricably linked with love for Christ. Our obedience stems from gratitude for what he has done for us on the cross; it is not a means of earning our salvation.

14:24   Jesus equates his words with the Father's words - he only speaks what the Father speaks.

Philippians 2:5-8

Jesus is our example of true obedience, willingly given.

Look at the definition of obedience and discuss how these verses help our understanding. God wants our willing obedience, given out of love for him, not just a cold submission to duty.

What are God's commands?

1 John 3:23-24

These verses encompass our duty to God and to our fellow man.

3:23   Belief in the name of Jesus Christ, God's Son. 'Jesus' means Saviour, 'Christ' is Messiah and 'God's Son' points to Jesus' divinity.

The second part is to love one another as Jesus commanded. How we do this will be looked at in detail in the coming weeks.

3:24   God's indwelling Holy Spirit is the guarantor of our salvation.

What are the consequences of disobedience?

Remind the group of the situation in the Garden of Eden (Genesis 2-3). God did not compel Adam and Eve's obedience, but warned them of the consequences of disobedience. God wants us to obey him willingly and warns us of the consequences if we do not.

1 Samuel 15:22-23

Paraphrase the story from verse 1. God's commands in verse 1-3 were very clear. Saul's disobedience was not due to mistaking God's will.

15:22   God rates obedience above empty religious observance.

15:23   Disobeying God is rebellion and putting myself in God's place.

These verses show how seriously God views disobedience.

Discipline

Discipline is the other part of the equation and is as important as exercise if we are not going to be flabby Christians. Ask the group to define 'discipline'. *Dictionary definition:- mental and moral training, adversity as affecting this.* Ensure the young people do not see 'discipline' as referring only to punishment.

Why is discipline necessary?

Without training chaos results, e.g. an untrained climbing plant, an untrained dog, an undisciplined child. Discipline is what keeps us going when we do not feel like it.

Hebrews 12:5-11

12:5-6	Proverbs 3:11-12. Note that it is a word of encouragement, addressed to Christians struggling to live a godly life (v.4).
12:7-8	Discipline is a sign of belonging to the family.
12:9	Discipline engenders respect for those in authority, (includes teachers, the law, the police, etc.).
12:10-11	Discipline helps us to lead a life that is pleasing to God.
	NB discipline is painful!

Self-discipline

The Hebrews passage talks about God's discipline. We need to look at self-discipline as well.

Titus 2:11-14

2:11	The grace of God includes all God's actions on our behalf - salvation and empowering us to live godly lives.
2:12	It is this grace that teaches us to say no to wrongdoing and to actively pursue right living.
	Self-control cannot be achieved by our own efforts alone (although effort is required!).
2:13	We must live in the present (v.12,14), but focussed on the future, looking forward to the day when Jesus will return in glory.

1. Whom should we obey? Look up the following verses and discuss what they mean in practice for your group. Ephesians 6:1-4, Hebrews 13:17, Romans 13:1-5.
2. We all fall short of God's standards, so what should we do when we fail? Look up 1 John 1:8-9. Is it enough just to say sorry without determining not to fail in that way again?
3. Read Acts 5:27-29. Is it ever right to disobey and, if so, in what circumstances?
4. How can self-discipline help keep us spiritually healthy?

Remember to encourage the group in daily Bible reading.

Play an adolescent version of 'Simon Says'. The group must obey all the commands that are preceded by 'Simon Says' and do nothing when commands are given without 'Simon Says'. Suggestions are: mime a pop singer, do 5 press-ups, perform a popular dance, etc.

Today we are learning about the importance of obedience in the normal Christian life.

PREPARATION

See Lesson Notes

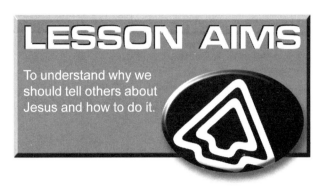

LESSON AIMS

To understand why we should tell others about Jesus and how to do it.

Introduction
Use the focus activity to introduce the concept of witness.

Why witness?

Matthew 28:16-20
Jesus commanded it. The great commission was given to Jesus' disciples (v.16) and is applicable to the church down through the ages.

28:19-20   The two essential ingredients for making disciples - baptism and teaching.

Romans 3:19-24
We are all under God's judgment and cannot save ourselves.

3:19   The word used for 'law' refers to the Scriptures as a whole. Those 'under the law' refers to the Jews. The Jews knew that the Gentiles were under God's judgment. Paul points out that they are too.

3:20   No one can keep the law fully, so no one can earn their own salvation.

An iimportant purpose of the law is to make us aware of our sinfulness.

3:21   As we cannot justify ourselves we need God's righteousness imputed to us.

3:22   Righteousness comes only through faith in Jesus Christ and is for **everyone** who believes.

Romans 10:14-17
People cannot believe the gospel if they have never heard it. Do the 'sent' in verse 15 mean only those people who have been sent by their church as missionaries or evangelists?

Who should witness?

Ephesians 4:11-13
These verses list different roles in the church, one of which is 'evangelist'.

1 Peter 3:13-16

3:13   Christians do get persecuted for following Christ (see v.14,16), but that persecution will not harm them ultimately. The Christian has a sure and certain hope - a place in heaven.

3:15   The way to counteract fear is to recognise Jesus as Lord. We must be prepared to answer other people's questions about the gospel.

How do we witness?

Romans 10:14-15
By word. But note how we are to do it - with gentleness and respect (1 Peter 3:15).

1 Peter 2:11-12
By godly living. The day of visitation is only used in the NT here and in Luke 19:44, where it refers to Jesus coming to Jerusalem with the offer of salvation. We never know when God will come to visit, offering salvation, and then the good deeds of the Christian will lead the pagan to glorify God by accepting his great salvation.

James 2:14
Our words must be backed up by our actions.

How to tell the gospel.
Use page 32 to teach the group a simple gospel outline. Photocopy it with the pictures covered and go through the outline adding the symbols as you go (see page 33).

FOCUS ACTIVITY

Divide the group into twos or threes and give each small group a copy of a recent newspaper. Ask them to find any reports of crimes or events where witnesses were involved. Feedback to the group what the witnesses saw or heard and how they described the crime or event. Why were the witnesses important? Did it matter if they reported things accurately?

Today we will learn why Jesus told people to be witnesses about him and who should do it.

QUESTIONS

1. What stops us witnessing to our friends? How can we encourage each other in this?
Make a list of 3 friends, who do not know the gospel, and ask God to give you the courage and opportunity to talk to them about Jesus.
2. Plan an evangelistic event to which you can invite people.
Remember to encourage the group in daily Bible reading.

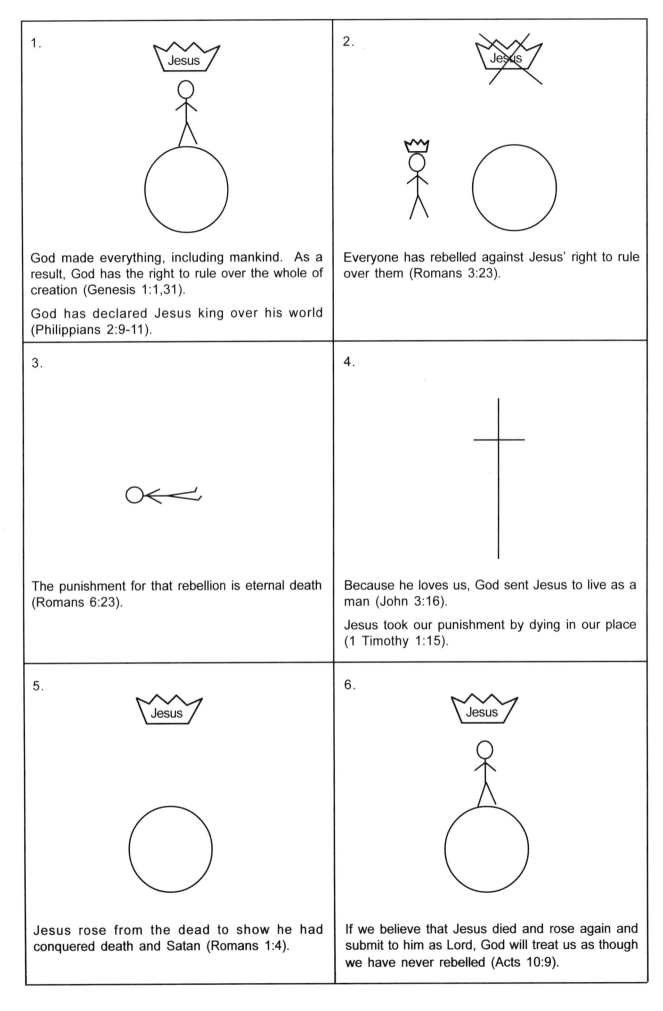

1.

God made everything, including mankind. As a result, God has the right to rule over the whole of creation (Genesis 1:1,31).

God has declared Jesus king over his world (Philippians 2:9-11).

2.

Everyone has rebelled against Jesus' right to rule over them (Romans 3:23).

3.

The punishment for that rebellion is eternal death (Romans 6:23).

4.

Because he loves us, God sent Jesus to live as a man (John 3:16).

Jesus took our punishment by dying in our place (1 Timothy 1:15).

5.

Jesus rose from the dead to show he had conquered death and Satan (Romans 1:4).

6.

If we believe that Jesus died and rose again and submit to him as Lord, God will treat us as though we have never rebelled (Acts 10:9).

1. Draw the circle (the world). Draw the man. Draw the crown (God ruling). Write 'Jesus' on the crown. God made everything, including mankind. As a result, God has the right to rule over the whole of creation (Genesis 1:1,31). God has declared Jesus king over his world (Philippians 2:9-11).	**2.** Draw the circle (the world). Draw the crown with 'Jesus' written on it. Draw the man to one side with a crown on. Place a cross over the Jesus crown. Everyone has rebelled against Jesus' right to rule over them (Romans 3:23).
3. Draw the man lying down (dead). The punishment for that rebellion is eternal death (Romans 6:23).	**4.** Draw the cross. Because he loves us, God sent Jesus to live as a man (John 3:16). Jesus took our punishment by dying in our place (1 Timothy 1:15).
5. Draw the circle (the world). Draw the crown with 'Jesus' written on it. Jesus rose from the dead to show he had conquered death and Satan (Romans 1:4).	**6.** Add in the man on top of the world to picture 5. The final picture is the same as the first one - as God intended. If we believe that Jesus died and rose again and submit to him as Lord, God will treat us as though we have never rebelled (Acts 10:9).

PREPARATION

See Lesson Notes

LESSON AIMS

To understand the importance of meeting with other Christians if we are to persevere in the Christian life.

Introduction

1. Focus activity.

2. Last session we looked at the importance of telling others about Jesus. Discuss whether or not they feel they can bring their friends to church / youth group. What stops them?

3. Let's have a look at what Christians do together - sometimes called 'fellowship'.

What is fellowship?

Ask the group to define fellowship.

In the NT the word used for 'fellowship' is also translated 'communion, communicate, partake, contribute'. It means sharing of something with someone and refers primarily to participation in something rather than association with others.

Look up the following verses and alter the group's definition accordingly: 1 Corinthians 1:9; 10:16, 2 Corinthians 8:3-4; 13:14, Philippians 2:1-2; 3:10.

In the OT the main use of the word 'fellowship' is for the fellowship offering, otherwise known as the peace offering (Leviticus 3:1-5; 7:11-15). Fellowship offerings were similar to the burnt offerings, but instead of the whole animal being burnt, only the fat and some of the inner parts were burnt on the altar. The rest was eaten as a fellowship meal and was shared by the worshippers and the priests. This fellowship meal was a way of remembering the peace between God and his chosen people.

Look up the following references to see what else we can learn about the way the Bible uses 'fellowship'.

1 Corinthians 5:1-2 - a group of believers.

Psalm 55:12-14 - a close relationship. In this psalm David is asking God for help in trouble, not only from his enemies (v.3), but also from his former friend. Note where the fellowship was enjoyed (v.14).

Acts 2:42-47 - a picture of the early church. Fellowship could mean a sharing of their possessions (v.44-45), but is more likely to be a shared meal or religious experience.

1 John 1:3-7 - fellowship with God and with each other should make a difference to the way we live. 'Walking in the light' means to live according to God's revelation in his word and not to prefer our own way. Following our own way, rather than God's, will put an obstacle in the way of our fellowship with each other.

Do we need fellowship?

Christianity is about relationships, first with God, then with others.

Hebrews 10:19-25

10:22   The first instruction is to draw near to God.

10:23   The second instruction is to hold firmly to our confidence in the new covenant. We can be certain of our forgiveness because we can trust God to keep his promises.

10:24   The third instruction is to encourage each other to love and do good deeds.

10:25   The fourth instruction is not to give up meeting together.

QUESTIONS

1. Can I be a solitary Christian (i.e. not go to church, meet with other Christians, etc.)?

2. In the light of today's study how should we structure our youth group meetings?

3. How can we encourage each other (Hebrews 10:24-25), not only at meetings but also throughout the week? (e.g. prayer, telephone, email)

4. How does this study help them decide on their priorities regarding time spent with Christian and non-Christian friends?

5. How far should the young people be incorporated into the general congregation? Is it acceptable for the youth group to be entirely separate, e.g. a youth church?

Remember to encourage the group in daily Bible reading.

FOCUS ACTIVITY

Sit the group in a circle and play the alphabet game based on things you do with friends. The first person must say something beginning with 'A', the second person something beginning with 'B', and so on. E.g. player 1 says 'aerobics', player 2 says 'basketball, player 3 says 'cinema', player 4 says 'drink coca cola', player 5 says 'eat', etc. Continue until 'Z' if possible.

This week we are learning about what Christians do together.

PREPARATION
See Lesson Notes

LESSON AIMS
To understand why God calls us to serve one another and to work out how we can do this in our situations.

Introduction

1. The Focus activity.

   Highlight the fun they had working together. What happened at the end? Who cleared up the mess? Point out that this is what happens often in our churches and youth groups - a lot of the work gets left for the few to do.

2. In school years 10 and 11 pupils often go on work experience. As a group think up as many work experience type jobs at your church as possible, e.g. photocopying, answering the telephone, cleaning, making coffee and tea, arranging flowers, child care, teaching Sunday School, counting the collection, banking money, property maintenance, moving furniture, tidying hymn books, etc.

3. Ask the group to define 'service'.
   Dictionary definition:- being a servant, done by a servant for a master.
   The word translated 'servant' in many modern translations also means 'slave' (Romans 1:1, Philippians 1:1, Titus 1:1, James 1:1). Servants/slaves had no rights in Bible times.

Whom should we serve?

1. God

Deuteronomy 10:12-13 - God's people (Israel) were commanded to serve God wholeheartedly. They were to walk in **all** God's ways and their service was not optional.

1 Peter 2:9-10 - we are part of God's people, so the above command applies to us.

2. One another

Romans 12:1-8 look at how the Christian should live in relationship with others.

12:1   A sacrifice had no rights - it was offered in its entirety.

      The act of worship is to do with the whole of life, not just for Sunday. The word translated 'worship' is used also for service.

12:2   Our minds are important and need to be renewed. We need a transformed world-view if we are to see our culture in the light of God's word.

12:3   We need humility, so that we do not think too highly of our own abilities.

12:4-6   Different people have different gifts. We must not compare ourselves with others and hanker after their gifts, but thank God for the ones he has given us.

12:6-8   Serving comes in the list of gifts, therefore it is essential for building up the body of Christ, the church. (See 1 Corinthians 12:4-7, where 'service' comprises several ministries.)

Why do we serve?
Ephesians 4:11-13 - to build up the body of Christ, the church.

Is service optional?
Is 'service' a special gift, like teaching or prophesying, so only for a select few?

Mark 10:42-45 - Jesus came to serve. The disciple is not greater than his master.

John 13:12-17 - Jesus' instructions to his disciples.

Philippians 2:1-4 - Paul's command to the Christians.

How should we serve?

Psalm 100:2 - with gladness (the word translated 'worship' in NIV is used also for service).

Ephesians 6:7 - wholeheartedly.

Philippians 2:3 - humbly, thinking of others as better than myself.

1 Peter 4:7-11 - using all the gifts God has given to us.

QUESTIONS

1. In the light of these verses how should we treat one another? How easy is it to think of others as better than myself?

2. What are the opportunities for service in our church fellowship? (Consider practical things, such as giving (money, hospitality, etc.), waiting on tables at a church evangelistic dinner, as well as jobs highlighted in the introduction.)

3. Is it enough just to do the jobs I find personally fulfilling? What about the more mundane jobs?

Remember to encourage the group in daily Bible reading.

FOCUS ACTIVITY

Divide the group into teams and give each team a toilet roll. The team members stand in line and pass the toilet roll over their heads from front to back without it breaking. Once the toilet roll reaches the back person it is passed back to the front by passing it through the team members' legs. The first team to complete the exercise **without breaking the toilet roll** wins.

Point out that team members had to work together in order to complete the exercise successfully. Ask the teams to divest themselves of the toilet paper and sit down. A leader clears up the mess.

PREPARATION

See
Lesson Notes

LESSON AIMS

To understand the work of the indwelling Holy Spirit in progressive sanctification.

Introduction

1. Focus activity.
2. Ask the group what sort of things they should do to stay healthy? Include such things as adequate diet, sufficient fluid intake, personal hygiene, recreation, sufficient rest/sleep, exercise, and record them on a board or flipchart.
3. Why is physical health so important? Sickness→impairment of efficiency→death. Is spiritual health important? What is necessary for spiritual health? Record their answers on the board or flipchart, including the following: Bible reading, prayer, obedience, discipline, witness, fellowship, service. If we work hard and do all these things, is it enough?

What makes me a Christian?

What I do or what Jesus has done?

Titus 3:4-8

3:5   We are saved through God's mercy, not by any merit of our own (see also v.7). 'washing of rebirth' probably refers to salvation (cf. John 3:3), although some commentators think the 'washing' refers solely to baptism.
'Renewal by the Holy Spirit' - this is ongoing. The Holy Spirit makes the believer a new person (cf. 2 Corinthians 3:17-18; 5:17, Romans 12:1-2).

3:6-7   The Holy Spirit indwells every believer (Romans 8:9).

3:8   The fact that good deeds do not save us does not mean that the Christian need not do good.

How does the Holy Spirit help me to live a godly life?

In the NT one of the Greek words used to describe the Holy Spirit is 'dunamos', which means the ability to get things done. It is usually translated as 'power' and is the root of the English words 'dynamo' and 'dynamite'.

2 Corinthians 3:17-18

The Holy Spirit transforms us from within to make us more like Jesus. This is an on-going work that lasts the whole of our lives.

Galatians 5:16-26

5:16   The Spirit is the Holy Spirit.
The sinful nature or flesh means our condition as fallen human beings.

5:17   The conflict between the Spirit and the flesh will continue until we die (see Romans 7:21-25).

5:18   The Holy Spirit is present in the lives of all believers (Romans 8:9) and, as a result, we are delivered from the penalty of the law. His ongoing work in the believer is one of sanctification (2 Corinthians 3:17-18). This verse does not mean that we do not need to keep God's law.

5:19-21 Our sinful nature is evidenced by our actions.

5:19   Deals with sexual sin.

5:20   Idolatry - offences against God. Witchcraft - any involvement with the powers of evil.

5:20-21 Hatred through to envy deal with a breakdown in society and personal relationships.

5:21   Drunkenness and orgies are to do with the abuse of alcohol and resultant loss of self-control.

Note the warning at the end of verse 21.

5:22-23 The fruit of the Spirit. The presence of the Holy Spirit in our lives is evidenced by our behaviour. Love, joy and peace are concerned primarily with our relationships with God and are all signs of the new birth - love for God, the joy of knowing we are forgiven and peace with God. Patience, kindness and goodness are primarily concerned with our relationships with other people. Patience means longsuffering, kindness is graciousness and gentleness, and goodness is doing good to others. Faithfulness, gentleness and self-control are primarily concerned with us. Faithfulness is dependability, loyalty and reliability, gentleness is meekness and absence of arrogance, and self-control is the opposite of Galatians 5:19-21.

Remember that, just as physical fruit grows slowly and steadily, so should spiritual fruit.

5:24   This verse does not imply that the Christian should not be troubled by the sinful nature, rather that he should set his face against the desires of the sinful nature, i.e. wage war against it.

5:25   'Keep in step with the Spirit'. The verb used for 'keep in step' comes from the same root as the noun used for the 'basic principles' that control us in Galatians 4:3,9. To keep in step with the Spirit is to allow his voice to be the controlling one and to seek to live by the principles laid down in Scripture.

5:26   Living by the Spirit should show itself in our dealings with each other. 'Provoke' is to challenge to a contest with the aim of demonstrating our own superiority, i.e. making others feel small and unimpressive. Provoking and envying come as a result of conceit.

1. Look up the following Bible verses:
    Acts 1:8; 6:1-4, Romans 8:15,26-27, 1 Corinthians 2:10-14; 12:4-7, Galatians 5:22-26, Ephesians 6:17-18, 1 Peter 1:12, 1 John 3:23-24.

    With reference to the categories covered in the series, how does the Holy Spirit enable me to live as a Christian?

2. If the Holy Spirit is the power source that enables me to live the Christian life, is there anything for me to do? (See Galatians 5:24-25.)

    Remember to encourage the group in daily Bible reading.

Divide the young people into twos or threes and give each group a pair of scissors and a selection of newspapers and magazines. Ask them to cut out any article or advertisment that has to do with being healthy. Pin the cut-outs onto a board and group them into categories, such as diets and dietary aids, exercise, skin care, etc. Discuss how society is taken up with being healthy, e.g. T.V. programmes, magazines, diets, etc.

OVERVIEW
Revelation

Week 13
Introduction Revelation 1:1-20
To get an overall view of the book and the language used in apocalyptic literature.

Week 14
The Letters to the Seven Churches Revelation 2:1 - 3:22
To understand what was good and bad about the churches in Asia and to apply the lessons learned to our own church situation.

Week 15
Wars Revelation 4:1 - 6:17
To understand that God is all powerful and is in control of everything.

Week 16
Disasters Revelation 7:1 - 11:19
1. To learn that the church will be persecuted right to the end.
2. To understand that final judgment is being delayed in order to allow men everywhere to hear the gospel and repent.

Week 17
Persecutions Revelation 12:1 - 14:20
1. To learn that, however powerful Satan appears, his time is shortlived and Christ has already won the victory over him.
2. To understand that no-one can sit on the fence - you have to choose between worshipping God or Satan.

Week 18
The End of the World Revelation 15:1 - 16:21
To understand that when God comes in judgment it will be too late to repent.

Week 19
The End of Evil Revelation 17:1 - 19:21
To understand that evil is not all powerful and Christ is victor.

Week 20
The End of Satan Revelation 20:1-15
1. To understand that judgment will be final.
2. To learn about the different views held by Christians about the Millennium.

Week 21
The World to Come Revelation 21:1 - 22:21
To learn how wonderful it will be to be for ever with the Lord, and how we should live in the light of his imminent return.

Recommended reading

Paul Barnett *Apocalypse Now and Then* The Anglican Information Office, Sydney
Michael Wilcock *The Message of Revelation* The Bible Speaks Today, IVP (1991)

SERIES AIMS

1. To understand how to read and interpret apocalyptic literature.

2. To understand what has and will happen to the church in the time before Jesus comes again, so that they are not taken by surprise.

3. To understand that the battle against Satan and evil was won at the cross. Their job is to remain faithful witnesses, in spite of persecution (Matthew 10:22, Mark 13:13).

MEMORY WORK

Weeks 13-17
Those whom I love I rebuke and discipline, so be earnest and repent.

Revelation 3:19

Weeks 18-21
All men will hate you because of me, but he who stands firm to the end will be saved.

Mark 13:13

Revelation

The Greek word translated 'Revelation' means unveiling something hidden, so that it may be seen and known for what it is. The book is difficult to understand because it abounds in symbolism of a type that we do not use and to which we no longer possess the key. Yet this kind of imagery was readily comprehensible to the men of the day, thus the author does not bother to explain it, which adds to our difficulties!

A. The Author

The author is John, son of Zebedee, one of Jesus' apostles. This was attested by both Justin Martyr, who wrote 50 years later, and Iranaeus, who wrote 80 years later. John lived in Ephesus for many years, so would have had the extensive knowledge of the area demonstrated by the author, e.g. the letters to the 7 churches were written in the order that a messenger would have travelled between them, according to the network of roads in the area. Some of the writing in the book is similar to John's gospel in its allusions, e.g. Revelation 21:6 cf. John 7:37; 4:14. However, there is a difference in the 2 writing styles, which is why some commentators have queried John the apostle's authorship of Revelation.

B. Apocalyptic Literature

The Revelation is the only complete book of this type in Scripture, although apocalyptic passages are found in other books, e.g. Matthew 24, the visions in Daniel, the visions in Ezekiel. This type of literature is characterised by the thought that God is sovereign and that ultimately he will intervene in catastrophic fashion to bring to pass his good and perfect will. He is opposed by powerful and varied forces of evil, which are usually referred to symbolically. It is very easy to get caught up in the detail and to end up with all sorts of weird and wonderful ideas. We need to look at the broader view of the visions and forget about trying to tie down the symbolism. As someone has said, we must look at Revelation as a picture book, not as a puzzle book.

C. Interpretation

The interpreters of Revelation fall into 3 main groups, according to the answer they give to the question: 'To what period of time do the visions and events of the book belong?'

1. Time Past

The book describes what was happening in the author's day and his conviction that God would intervene to put it right. The prophecies had their fulfilment by the early part of the 4th century.
This ignores the teaching on the second coming.

2. Time Future

From chapter 4 onwards the events depicted are concerned solely with the end time (the second coming of Christ). Chapters 2 and 3 are thought by some futurists to portray the moral history of the church in 7 successive periods of history from the close of the first century AD.
This view removes the book entirely from its historical setting, so it is not easy to see what meaning it would have had for its first readers.

3. Comprehensive/historical

The book contains a panoramic view of history from the 1st century until the second coming. Adherents of this view fall into 3 groups -

a) The book sets out the chief phases of church history. The problem with this view is that they cannot agree which vision portrays which phase of history.

b) The book sets out history without a break, i.e. the visions follow on one after another chronologically. There is the same problem as with a). Also, there are obvious examples of parallelism in the book, so that it cannot be a continuous view of history without a break.

c) The book is concerned with the broad sweep of the unfolding of the kingdom of God to its great climax, the second coming. This seems to be the most logical way of interpretation. Revelation presents the great drama of the conflict between Christ and his people on the one hand, and Satan and his followers on the other. It covers the unfolding of the entire history of Christ's kingdom from the beginning of the Christian era to the grand climax at the second coming.

D. Understanding Revelation

1. Use of symbols

The book is full of symbols and most of it is written in sign language. John was in the Spirit on the Lord's day and successive visions passed before his eyes. Compare Peter's vision in Acts 10 where a great sheet is let down by 4 corners, in which were all kinds of birds, beasts and insects. Everything in the sheet was ritually unclean, so could not be eaten by a Jew. God's command to Peter to rise and eat brings him to the realisation that God is no respector of persons and will freely receive Gentiles who believe, as well as believing Jews. So it is with the visions seen by John. John is teaching using pictures, not wordy explanations, and the symbols are not to be taken literally.

Paul Barnett, in *Apocalypse Now and Then*, gives the following meaning for some of the symbols:

white, throne, crown	conquest and kingly rule
horn	power
eye	knowledge
right hand	authority
land beast/false prophet	Roman provincial governors
sea beast and harlot	Roman emperor and his government

2. Significant numbers

The numbers in Revelation are also used symbolically:

3	a sacred number (the trinity).
3½	(42 months) is half of 7 (see below) and points to a period of history that is finite, not eternal like God.
4	a number of completion (4 sides to a square).
6	the number of man (man created on the 6th day), hence the 666 in Revelation 13:18.
7	the number of completeness and perfection, e.g. seven spirits in Revelation 1:7 = the perfect Spirit of God. This number is also used to signify eternity (seventh day of rest).
12	the elective purposes of God (12 tribes, 12 apostles). Thus 24 is the number of the leaders from Old and New Covenants.
1000	sacred number 3 added to number of perfection to form 10, the number of completeness, then cubed. It speaks of the completeness and perfection of Christ's victory over Satan. It also means a great number or long period of time.
144,000	12 (number of election) squared and multiplied by 1000. Symbolises the full number of saints of both covenants who are preserved by God.

3. Structure of the book

a) 1:1-20   Introduction and vision 1.

b) 2:1 - 3:22   The 7 letters arising from vision 1.

c) 4:1 - 20:15   Vision 2 dealing with the journey of God's people from the foundation of the church to the second coming of Jesus. This can be split into 6 sections, in each of which John leads up to the second coming, then starts again at an earlier point. 1 section will be dealt with each week. There is a considerable amount of parallelism between the various sections.

d) 21:1 - 22:21   The new heavens and the new earth.

Between chapters 5 and 16 there are 4 episodes that look at the destiny of believers through history. Each episode consists of 7 elements, which show them to be ordained by God (7 being the perfect number). After the 6th element in each episode there is an interlude followed by the 7th element, which acts as a bridge to the next episode. The episodes do **not** follow on chronologically, but run concurrently, therefore, it is unhelpful to try and locate them in specific periods of history. All 4 episodes occur right through the period stretching from Jesus' resurrection to his second coming.

4. Jesus is the centre

The book should **not** be read as though its main teaching is about the Battle of Armageddon, but in the light of Jesus' completed victory on the cross. The battle against Satan is not in the future, it has already been fought and won! There is no description of Jesus' second coming in the book, but it is everywhere presupposed or alluded to.

5. The Use of Parallelism

In parts of the book John parallels aspects of Roman society in a negative way with elements of the gospel, e.g. the harlot (ch.17) with the godly woman (chs.12 & 21), Babylon (ch.18) with the new Jerusalem (ch.21-22), the beast with a mortal wound (13:3) with the lamb that is slain (13:8), the mark on the foreheads of the worshippers of the beast (13:15-17) with the mark on the foreheads of the worshippers of the lamb (22:3-4), the characteristics of the beast's followers (21:8; 22:15) with the characteristics of the church (14:4-5).

6. The Use of Language

Language used in different ways throughout the Bible:

- literal statements,
- symbolism,
- metaphor.

Discuss with the group the statement *Israel was a land flowing with milk and honey.*

Do they take it literally? - i.e. when the children of Israel entered Canaan they walked into a sticky mess of milk and honey flowing over the ground.

Do they take is symbolically? - i.e. milk = God's word and honey = Holy Spirit.

So, how do they understand it? - a fertile land full of good things, plenty of food, etc. (metaphorically).

Now look at the structure of the sentence.

Israel was a land - a literal statement.

milk and honey - literal.

flowing - metaphorical.

Hence in Revelation 9:7-10; 14:20 the literal interpretation is absurd. The details are given to show the fearsomeness and gruesomeness of the things portrayed.

For group members who want to take it all literally, the following approach is suggested:

a) Discuss the milk and honey sentence. Do they take that literally? If not, why not?

b) Look at the beast with 7 heads and 10 horns (Revelation 13:1) and the woman with a posterior large enough to sit on 7 hills (17:3-9). Do they take that literally? If not, why not?

c) Get them to state which bits they do take literally and explain what it is about those bits that makes them literal when the rest is symbolic.

d) Look at 2 Timothy 3:15-17. Ask them to explain to you how a literal interpretation of Revelation helps them in their daily walk with God.

E. Contemporary Problems

In John's day the church faced several problems

1. Jewish Antagonism

Following the destruction of the temple in Jerusalem in AD 70, the Jews paid the temple tax to Rome. As a result they were exempt from the requirement to worship the Emperor, which was placed on all people in the Roman Empire. By the time Revelation was written, the Christians were no longer considered to be a Jewish sect, so were not given the same exemption. The local Jewish population probably denounced the Christians to the local authority (Revelation 2:9; 3:9). This made the Christians subject to persecution by the authorities, which had started as early as the time of Nero (AD 60s), following the expulsion of the Jews from Rome.

2. Heretical Infiltration

The church was already being led astray by heretical teachings, e.g. the Nicolaitans (2:6,15) and the teaching of Balaam (2:14,20). See Week 14 for details of these teachings.

3. Caesar Worship

Syncretism (the worship of more than one god), involvement in magic and the occult, and sexual laxity were the norm in Roman society. The Emperor was spoken of as a god and saviour and beautiful temples were built in which statues of Caesar were worshipped. Whom you worshipped was the test of true conviction and loyalty. For the Christian, saying yes to God meant saying no to all alternatives, when refusing to worship Caesar could mean death.

This is a lesson our young people need to learn. Our society is very similar to the Roman society of John's day and it is very hard for Christians to be uncompromising in their worship of God.

PREPARATION

Revelation 1:1-20

LESSON AIMS

To get an overall view of the book and the language used in apocalyptic literature.

Some of the series overview (e.g. use of language, numbers, symbolism) needs to be covered in order to sort out how the book is to be studied. It is helpful to pick out the attributes of Jesus mentioned in Chapter 1, as these are used in the 7 letters and elsewhere in the book.

1:1 The author is John, God's servant, your brother (v.9), one of the prophets (22:9). He is thought to be John the apostle, author of the gospel and the 3 epistles (see series overview). The book was written at a time when the church was undergoing persecution and difficulty (cf. v.9), which could be either during the reign of Nero or Domitian. The inclination today is towards the latter view, because the churches written to in chapters 2-3 had become complacent and were declining spirituality, whereas the church in Nero's day was younger and more vigorous. This would make the time of writing about AD 96.

The angel sent to John may have been a human messenger with news from the 7 churches (see, *Apocalypse Now and Then* by Paul Barnett, p.38).

1:3 The book is a prophecy.

1:4-5 Note the trinitarian reference:

- the Father (the one who is, was and is to come)

- the Spirit (the 7 spirits, see series overview for use of numbers)

- the Son (Jesus Christ).

1:5 This verse encompasses a gospel statement. Jesus is the faithful witness (through his death), the firstborn from the dead (resurrection), and the ruler (ascended). Jesus is ruler because he is the Lamb who was slain (5:6).

1:6 Cf. 1 Peter 2:9.

1:7 Cf. Daniel 7:13 and Zechariah 12:10. This verse demonstrates Jesus' divinity by picking up Messianic statements from the OT.

1:8 Alpha and omega are the first and last letter of the Greek alphabet. This term was probably used to express the entirety of a thing. It also expresses God's lordship over history (see also Exodus 3:14). Almighty = all powerful.

1:9-18 **John's first vision**

1:10 Being in the Spirit could mean either prophesying to other Christians on Patmos, or being engaged in some form of meditation.

1:11 7 is the number of perfection and completeness, signifying that the letters are to the whole church (see also 'he who has an ear', etc. at the end of each letter). The 7 churches named lay on a route forming a sort of inner circle around the province of Asia (see map of the area). They would have been ideal centres for circulating the letters to other churches.

1:12 See v.20 for the meaning of the lamp stands.

1:13 Cf. Daniel 7:13.

1:13-16 Cf. Daniel 10:5-6; 7:9. Note the application of the attributes of God to Christ.

1:16 For the meaning of the 7 stars see v.20. The double edged sword represents judicial authority and might. Note that it comes from his mouth (God's word), cf. Hebrews 4:12.

1:19 'What you have seen' is the vision just given plus the news about the existing state of the churches and the letters to be written.

'What is now' is the reality of Jesus' conquering death on the cross (chs.4-5).

'What you will see hereafter' is the subsequent visions of the book (chs.6-20).

1:20   No-one is sure what the angels are. It seems unlikely that they are angels in the usual meaning of the term - why would God use John to write to angels (2:1, etc.)? Some people think they represent officials in the churches, but nowhere else in scripture do angels represent men, apart from possibly in v.3. However, the term does mean 'messenger' in the OT, so these 'angels' could well be the teaching elder(s) in the congregations, responsible for the spiritual life and well-being of the flock.

See map on page 49

Photocopy page 48 for each group member. The missing word is 'earnest' (3:19).

1. Why did God reveal to John what was to happen?

2. What terms are used to describe Jesus in this passage? How do they help our understanding of who Jesus is and what he has accomplished?

FOCUS ACTIVITY

Pictionary Divide the group into teams. The leader stands at some distance from the teams with a list of words taken from the passage: a lampstand, robe, feet, snow, stars, sword, etc. A member of each team comes to the leader to be given a word and returns to their team to draw it without using words or letters. No speech or hand gestures can be used. When someone in the team correctly guesses the word they go to the leader for the next word. Continue until all the words have been used.

Link to the study by stating that Revelation is an exciting book all about Jesus Christ. Like the pictures they have drawn, often it may not look as though it is about Jesus (you may want to refer to some of the pictures they have drawn!), but the beginning verse of Revelation tells us that it is. If we remember this it will help us to understand the book as we study it.

Fill the names of the seven churches into the grid below in such a way that the shaded column spells the missing word from the memory verse.

EPHESUS   SMYRNA   PERGAMUM   THYATIRA
SARDIS   PHILADELPHIA   LAODICEA

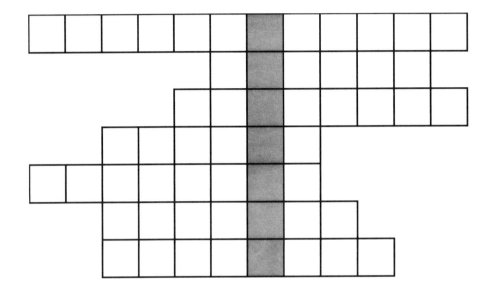

Those whom I love I rebuke and discipline, so be .... and repent.

Revelation 3:19

To which church was this addressed?

The Seven Churches

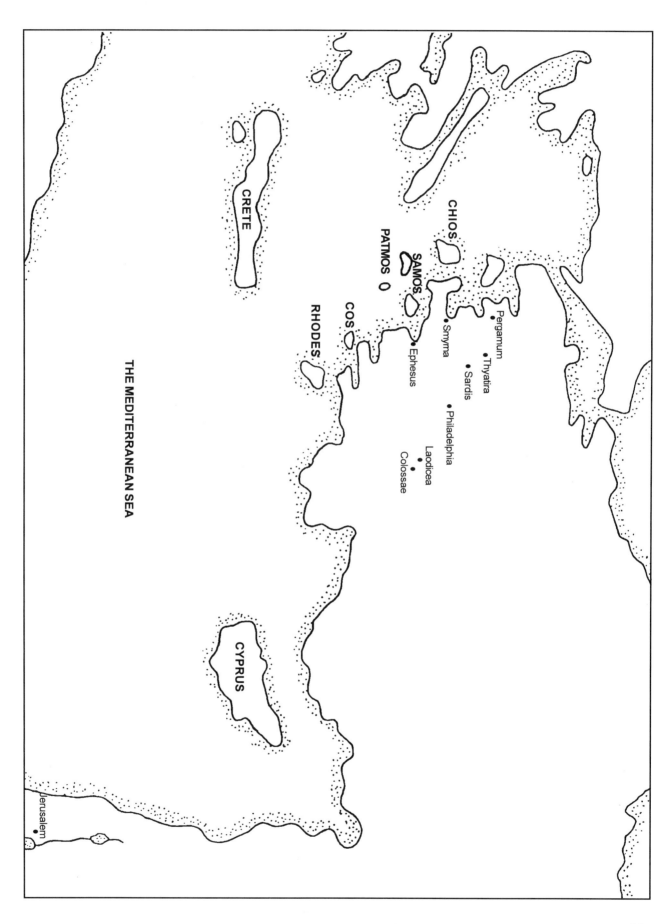

WEEK 14
The Letters to the
Seven Churches

PREPARATION
Revelation 2:1 - 3:22

LESSON AIMS
To understand what was good and bad about the churches in Asia and to apply the lessons learned

In order to cover all 7 letters in one study the following approach is suggested:

1. What title is given to Jesus in each letter?- these are taken from chapter 1.

2. What is commended in each church?

3. What is wrong in each church?

4. What is commanded?

5. What is given to him who overcomes?

The letters follow the same pattern:
- directed to the angel (messenger)
- the words are from Jesus
- praise for what they are doing well
- censure for what they are doing wrong
- a call to repent
- encouragement and a promise for the future.

2:1-7 Ephesus

2:1   Ephesus was a port and an important trade centre. It was also the centre for worship of the goddess Artemis (see Acts 19:35).

2:6   The Nicolaitans were reputed to be followers of Nicolaus of Antioch, one of the 7 (Acts 6:5). We gather from 2:14-15 that they held the same error as the Balaamites, i.e. luring the believers to eat food sacrificed to idols and to commit fornication (see Numbers 25:1-3; 31:16).

2:7   'He who has an ear' indicates that the teaching of the letter is relevant to all who read it.

        The tree of life, see 22:2, Genesis 2:9. The Ephesians revered a sacred tree near the temple of Artemis. This temple offered asylum to anyone requiring it, so became a centre for criminals. As a result of this the tree at Ephesus was at the centre of a band of those same evil doers that will be outside the new Jerusalem (22:14-15).

2:8-11 Smyrna

2:8   Smyrna was another port and trade centre. It was renowned for its architecture and was a very beautiful city.

2:9   The Jews were protected by law from taking part in pagan religious ceremonies, but the Christians were not. This verse implies that the Jews were denouncing the Christians to the authorities. John states these Jews are not 'real' Jews, i.e. they are not part of God's people (cf. Galatians 3:6-9).

2:10   10 days = a short period.

        The crown of life alludes to the wreath bestowed on the winner in the games.

2:11   The second death - see 21:8.

2:12-17 Pergamum

2:12   Pergamum was an inland city and was not as wealthy as Ephesus or Smyrna. It was the capital of Roman Asia.

2:13   Emperor worship was established in Pergamum earlier than at Ephesus or Smyrna and Pergamum became recognised as the centre of the cult in Asia. There were also many heathen temples on the hill overlooking the city, hence, 'where Satan has his throne'.

2:14-15 See notes on 2:6.

2:17   There was a current Jewish expectation that manna would descend from heaven again when the Messiah was manifested. Manna typifies spiritual life, cf. the water of life (22:17). Part of Emperor worship was to eat a ceremonial meal as a token of loyalty to the State.

        The white stone is difficult to interpret, owing to the multitude of uses to which stones were put, e.g. following a jury trial a white stone indicated innocence, a black stone indicated guilt. Stones may also have been used as entry tickets to the gladiator arena.

A new name was bestowed on persons who had attained new status, e.g. Abram - Abraham, Jacob - Israel. The phrase, therefore, probably signifies the right of the newcomer to enter God's kingdom as an individual, through God's grace.

2:18-29 Thyatira

2:18   Thyatira was the least important of the 7 cities. It was an industrial city, renowned for its many trade guilds. To carry on business it was necessary to be a member of a guild, with all that this entailed, e.g. common meals where food had been offered to idols. Lydia came from Thyatira (Acts 16:14).

2:20   Jezebel was instrumental in introducing pagan worship into Israel (see 1 Kings 16:31, 2 Kings 9:22). In this verse the woman was from among the congregation and the false teaching was the same as the Balaamites (cf. vv.6,14-15).

2:22-23   It is unclear whether this verse should be interpreted literally or metaphorically. What is certain is that God will come in righteous judgment and no-one will escape.

2:24   Satan's deep secrets may refer to the various guild initiation rites.

2:26   See Revelation 19:11-16.

2:28   Balaam spoke of a star arising from Jacob (Numbers 24:17). Jesus is the morning star (2 Peter 1:19).

3:1-6 Sardis

3:4   White robes symbolise moral purity (see also 7:13-14). Soiled clothes indicate moral and spiritual compromise.

3:5   See Revelation 20:12,15.

3:7-13 Philadelphia

3:7   Philadelphia, owing to frequent earthquakes, had a small population. People had to leave frequently to escape earthquake devastation, then returned to rebuild. This meant that life was very uncertain. Philadelphia was the centre of the grape growing region, but in AD 92 the Emperor banned grape growing in order to promote greater corn production. This also caused people to move away from the area.

3:8   The open door could refer to the believer's access to God through Jesus (Hebrews 4:14-16), or to missionary outreach. Philadelphia was situated at the limit of civilisation and the road led from there to the interior.

3.12   God will be the temple (see 21:22), therefore this speaks of the believer's unity with God. It was common practice to dedicate a temple pillar to honour a prominent citizen.

3:14-22 Laodicea

3:14   Laodicea was a large commercial and administrative centre. It was a banking centre, a centre for the manufacture of clothing and woollen carpets, and had a medical school.

3:15-16   There were lukewarm mineral springs in nearby Heirapolis, where people went to take the waters. They tasted foul.

3:17   Following a major earthquake, the people refused outside help from the Emperor and rebuilt the city themselves, which was a source of immense pride.

3:18   The medical school was renowned for its eye ointment.

3:20   Jesus will give them everything they need (cf. Philippians 4:19).

3:21   See 22:5.

1. Each letter ends with an injunction to hear what the Spirit says to the churches. List what was commended in each church, what was reproved and what was commanded. How do these lists help us to understand the strong and weak points in our youth fellowship?

Map (see page 49).

Run Around   To get the young people looking at quite a large passage, run a quiz about the seven churches. Designate 7 church stations around the room, each representing a different church (Ephesus, Pergamum, Thyatira, etc.). All the young people stand in the middle of the room, each one with a Bible open at Revelation 2-3. Ask the group a question about one of the churches, such as:

♦ Who has forgotten their first love?
♦ In which church are some walking in white clothes, yet some are dead on their feet?
♦ Which church was told, 'I am going to spit you out of my mouth!'?

The young people look in their Bibles to find out which church is referred to and run to that station. The last person there is given a point. At the end of the quiz the person with least points is the winner.

Link in to the study by pointing out that these 7 churches in Asia received letters from Jesus, written by John. Some churches were doing better than others, but all of them had improvements to make or suffer the consequences. As we look at these letters, God may teach us a few things about our own church!

Divide into small units of three or four and ask them to write a letter to the whole group. What sort of letter would God write to our group? What would be commended? What would be reproved? What would be commanded? Comments must **not** be about individuals, but about the group as a whole. Compare the letters and discuss what action should be taken by the group as a result.

PREPARATION

Revelation 4:1 - 6:17

LESSON AIMS

To understand that God is all powerful and is in control of everything.

As you read these chapters visualise John's description and work out what the picture says. **Chapter 4** describes God on his throne in heaven in all his majesty and power, continually worshipped by the 24 elders and 4 living creatures.

4:1   The word used for 'standing open' means that the door is **always** open.

4:2   John was conscious that his vision was from God.

4:3   This verse describes God's kingly rule. The throne symbolises conquest and the rainbow mercy (see Genesis 9:15-16).

4:4   The 24 elders are the heavenly representatives of God's people. 24 could refer to the 12 tribes plus 12 apostles, i.e. the saved from both dispensations. Thrones, white clothes and crowns symbolise their victory as witnesses, having endured opposition.

4:5   The thunder and lightning symbolise judgment. The 7 spirits is the complete, perfect Spirit of God.

4:6   The sea of glass - see 15:2. The 4 living creatures - see Ezekiel 1:4-28. The Jews interpreted Ezekiel's vision as portraying the subjection of all nature to God - man is the chief representative of creatures, the eagle of birds, the lion of beasts, and the ox of cattle. The many eyes indicate much knowledge.

4:8   Repeating a word 3 times is the superlative form in Hebrew. We have 'holy', 'holier' (comparative) and 'holiest' (superlative). Hebrew has 'holy', 'holy, holy' and 'holy, holy, holy', signifying the most holy of all. The 4 living creatures make a gospel statement (see 14:6-7), which is responded to in worship by the 24 elders (v.10-11).

4:10-11   True worship is the people of God celebrating a truth about God - who he is and what he does.

Chapter 5 describes Jesus, in heaven with God, worshipped as God is worshipped.

5:1   A scroll with 7 seals was a testament, opened after the death of the testator in the presence of the 7 witnesses who sealed it.

5:2   The scroll can only be opened by one worthy to execute it.

5:4   Unless the scroll is opened what it contains will not come to pass.

5:5   See Genesis 49:8-12, Isaiah 11:1-5. The Messiah was from the tribe of Judah and a descendant of David. He has triumphed through his death and resurrection. The verb used for triumphed is in the past tense, stating that this conquest has already taken place. It is complete and unlimited.

5:6   The Lamb - see Isaiah 53:7, John 1:35-36, 1 Corinthians 5:7. The horn symbolises power (Psalm 75:4-5, Zechariah 1:18-19). 7 is the number of completeness/perfection, so 7 horns indicate divine power. 7 eyes indicate omniscience. In the OT this quality belongs to God (Zechariah 4:10). Only God has divine knowledge and is worthy of worship (v.9-10).

5:9   The Lamb is worthy of worship because his blood purchased redemption.

5:13   See Philippians 2:9-11.

Chapter 6 describes the first of 4 sequences concerning what is to happen on the earth prior to the second coming of Jesus. Each sequence is in 7 parts, 6 plus an interlude. Each interlude leads into the next sequence. The 4 sequences deal with wars (chs.6-7), disasters (chs.8-11), persecution (chs.12-14) and the destruction of evil (chs.15-16). These all go on simultaneously throughout the time from Jesus' resurrection until his second coming. John deals with them in turn so we can understand what is happening and learn from it.

6:2 Conquest. White and the crown symbolise conquest and kingly rule, the bow symbolises warfare.

6:3-4 War. Conquest always leads on to warfare.

6:5-6 Famine, hunger and disease always follow on warfare. Note that a handful of wheat cost a day's wages. God's mercy is seen in the preservation of the oil and the wine.

6:7-8 Death through war, famine, plague and wild animals. God's mercy is demonstrated in the horseman only being allowed to kill a set number. These 4 always follow on naturally. Conquest always results in the other 3. John was probably referring to Rome. Note that the horses only come because God allows them to (the Lamb broke the seals and the living creatures said, 'Come').

6:9-11 Christian martyrs ask how long before the judgment and are told to wait until the number of the saved, who were to be martyred as they had been, was completed. This speaks of God's sovereignty. Christians were persecuted by Rome in John's day and are being persecuted today. Tyrants always persecute those who withhold their worship from them.

6:9 The altar was a place of protection (see also 8:3). The martyrs here are the same as those in 20:4.

6:11 The white robes symbolise victory. The time they have to wait is the age of the church, that whole period between Jesus' resurrection and his second coming.

6:12-17 The final judgment. See Matthew 24:29-31, Joel 2:31, Isaiah 34:2-4, Hosea 10:8, Joel 2:10-11.

That part of Asia was subject to massive earthquakes. The description of the destruction of Pompeii by the volcanic eruption of Mount Vesuvius in AD 79 is very similar to John's description in v.12-14.

6:15 All are included: rich/poor, slave/free.

What do we learn?

1. God is all powerful and is in control.

2. Jesus is God.

3. When God comes in judgment it will be too late to repent.

1. Who is being spoken about in 5:5? (See Genesis 49:8-12, Isaiah 11:1-5.) Why is it important to know that Jesus has **already** triumphed over Satan?

2. 6:9-11 speaks of God's sovereignty. How does this concept help us in our Christian lives?

What is God Like? A brainstorming activity. Ask the young people, 'What sort of words do people use today to describe God?' Write their answers on a board or flipchart. If you have time beforehand, you might want to ask a few people in the street and record their answers.

Let's see how these answers compare with John's vision of God. Divide the group into pairs and ask them to read quickly through Revelation 4:1-11 and see how this vision of God compares with what is written on the flipchart. Continue with the remainder of the Bible study.

Photocopy page 55 for each group member. The remaining word is 'Almighty'.

All the following words from today's Bible passage can be found in letter pairs in the grid. The words read either horizontally, vertically or diagonally and can read backwards or forwards, but the letter pairs will always read from left to right. No letter pair is used more than once. One word on the list has been done to show you. When you have found all the listed words you will be left with a word that describes God.

APPEARANCE	EARTHQUAKE	HONOUR	PRAISE	TRUE
BROTHERS	EYES	HOLY	SCALES	WEALTH
CONQUEST	FAMINE	LAMB	SCROLL	WISDOM
CROWNS	FOUR	LION	STRENGTH	WORSHIPPED
DOOR	GOLD	PLAGUE	THRONE	WORTHY

UR	LI	RS	HE	OT	BR	CR	GO	LD	ST
NO	ON	UE	ST	WI	SD	OM	OW	UE	WO
HO	AG	RE	NE	MI	FA	HY	NQ	NS	RS
PL	NG	EY	SC	KE	AL	CO	RT	PR	HI
TH	OR	ES	UA	AL	LL	MI	AI	WO	PP
LA	DO	HQ	FO	RO	ES	SE	GH	LY	ED
MB	RT	UR	SC	NE	RO	TH	TR	TY	HO
EA	AP	PE	AR	AN	CE	UE	TH	AL	WE

What is the remaining word?

PREPARATION

Revelation 7:1 - 11:19

LESSON AIMS

The church will be persecuted to the end. Final judgment is being delayed in order to allow men everywhere to hear the gospel and repent.

As you read try and visualise what John describes. It helps with understanding the overall message.

7:1-17 Interlude between 6th and 7th seals

7:1-8 The first part of the interlude takes place on earth. God's people are marked, i.e. known to him, and will be saved from eternal judgment. This does not mean that they will escape from suffering whilst on earth. God is in control!

7:1 'After this' indicates another vision, not something occurring chronologically after the events described at the end of chapter 6. The 4 angels have been given power to harm the earth. The winds are winds of destruction, but are restrained until the full number of the elect are sealed.

7:3 Cf. Ezekiel 9:3-6. The seal was the divine mark so that those sealed would escape divine judgement.

7:4 The 144,000 consist of 12,000 from each of the 12 tribes, therefore they represent the true Jews, i.e. the believers from the Old Covenant. Godly Jews under the Old Covenant enjoy the same protection as believers under the New Covenant (see v.9).

7:5-8 Manasseh was part of the tribe of Joseph and Dan is missing, so the numbers are not meant literally. They need to be taken in conjunction with v.4.

7:9-17 The second part of the interlude takes place in heaven.

7:9 This verse talks of people from every tribe and nation, therefore it refers to believers under the New Covenant. Palm branches indicate victory, as do the colour of the robes.

7:10,12 Note the gospel statement in v.10 is followed by a worship statement in v.12. This coupling of gospel and worship statements occurs several times in Revelation.

7:14 The 'great tribulation' refers not to Mark 13:14-20 (AD 70). It is the persecution from Nero until the second coming.

8:1-5 **The 7th seal**
This takes place in heaven. The prayers of the saints go up to God, judgment goes down from God to the earth.

8:2 7 angels with 7 trumpets speak of completeness and perfection. Trumpets were blown to herald the start of something, e.g. the Jewish New Year.

8:5 Cf. Exodus 19:16-19. Thunder and lightning are signs of God's presence.

8:6 - 11:19 The 7 trumpets are sounded, signifying different disasters. The interval between 6th and 7th trumpet, as between the 6th and 7th seal, indicates God's mercy in delaying final judgment so that all should have a chance to repent. But the final judgment will not be delayed indefinitely. When it comes it will be too late to repent.

8:7-12 **The first 4 trumpets**
These herald natural disasters on an unprecedented scale affecting all the natural order, earth, sea, waters, heavens. Note: only a third of everything is destroyed. This is not a literal number; a third indicates many, but not a majority. The comfort for Christians is that there is a limit set to the destruction. God is in control!

9:1-21 **The 5th and 6th trumpets**
These affect mankind.

9:1-12 The 5th Trumpet (cf. Joel 2:1-11). This trumpet heralds an attack that is on the non-Christian (v.4), is demon controlled (v.11), leads to despair (v.6), and will not affect the natural order (v.4).

9:1 The abyss is the domain of Satan. The falling star is not identified.

9:2-3	The disaster is supernatural and involves the torture of mankind (v.5).
9:5,10	5 months is the life cycle of some locusts. Here it indicates a period within history and a limitation set by God.
9:7-10	A picture of the fearsomeness and gruesomeness of the problem.
9:13-19	The 6th Trumpet. Plagues are let loose to kill a third of mankind. Again God is in control - limits are set to the number destroyed. This plague is heralded by 4 evil angels under the control of Satan.
9:13	The horns of the altar show that this judgment is direct from God. The prayers of the saints were offered at the altar (see 8:3). Prayer **is** effective, even though it appears weak in the eyes of the world.
9:14	The River Euphrates signified the boundary of the land of Israel (cf. Genesis 15:18). In John's day it bordered the civilised world, beyond which lived the Parthians - feared horsemen and warriors. Here it signifies that destruction comes from outside the church.
9:16	The number indicates a vast multitude.
9:17-18	A picture of how dreadful it will be. This colour of the breastplates corresponds to what is coming out of the horses' mouths, red for fire, blue for smoke and yellow for sulphur. Could this be a picture of different ideologies?
9:20-21	Those that are left are given the chance to repent of impure worship (v.19) and impure lives (v.20), but refuse. God is not willing that any should perish.
10:1-11:14	**Interlude between 6th and 7th trumpets** This interlude is also split into 2 parts, the call to prophesy (10:1-11) and the 2 prophets (11:1-14).
10:1-11	**The call to prophesy** The angel brings John a message for the world, one that is sweet to him as a Christian (Psalm 19:10), but bitter in what must be declared to those who oppose God (Jeremiah 15:16, Ezekiel 3:1-3). Disaster on its own does not cause men to repent (9:20-21). People need to be told **why** the disaster has happened and that it is a precursor of final judgment (explanation and interpretation).
10:1	The rainbow is a sign of God's mercy (Genesis 9:12-16).
10:6	No more delay, the mystery of God is about to be revealed. God's servants, the prophets, know what the mystery is, but need to be courageous enough to tell the world in the

	midst of disasters and persecutions. The mystery is the gospel (Ephesians 3:2-6).
10:10	To eat the scroll is to assimilate its contents (cf. Ezekiel 2:8 - 3:3,10,14). John accepts the commission to preach the gospel.
10:11	OT prophecy was directed at Israel. NT prophecy is directed at the world.
11:1-14	**The 2 Witnesses** John draws symbols from Ezekiel 40 - 41 (measuring the temple) and Zechariah 4 (the olive trees). The measuring indicated God's protection and care for his people. The 2 olives represent the church, faithful to death. (OT law required evidence to be attested by at least 2 witnesses, Deuteronomy 19:15). Working against the witnesses are the anti-God forces of the 'beast' with power to kill and dishonour, but not destroy or prevent triumph.
11:1	The temple, altar and worshippers refer to the company of believers and measuring symbolises protection.
11:2	The outer court refers to the rest of historical Jerusalem, which is outside the temple, and domain of the Gentiles. This is not measured (under God's protection). 42 months = 1260 days (v.3). This was the traditional apocalyptic time of Gentile domination derived from Daniel 9:27; 12:7, where its primary reference is to the defilement by Antiochus IV in 167-164 BC. John refers to the Roman destruction of Jerusalem (AD 70.) It indicates that God has set a limit to the duration of the trials - the exact time is unimportant.
11:3	The number of days refers to a long, but limited time. The 2 witnesses stand for churches (lamp stands, v.4, cf. 1:20) where God's word is proclaimed. They will prophesy for a lengthy, but limited time.
11:4	In Zechariah 4:2-14 the Jews recognised the 2 witnesses as Zerubbabel (the governor) and Joshua (the high priest). It stands for the church in its royal and priestly functions.
11:6	The powers given to the witnesses are those of Moses and Elijah - the law and the prophets (OT church).
11:7	The beast from the abyss is Satan.
11:8	Sodom and Egypt were by-words for evil and oppression. Jerusalem's treatment of Jesus demonstrated hostility to God. The 'great city' here stands for any city where Christians are persecuted.

11:11	The reference to the resurrection of the witnesses probably refers to the first resurrection, i.e. they are in heaven with Jesus, part of the multitude who lost their lives due to martyrdom.
11:12	God's holy place is now in heaven, not on earth. The historical Jerusalem has no further theological significance.
11:13	John may be referring to circumstances surrounding the martyrdom of specific individuals. The whole region of Asia, where the 7 churches were situated, was prone to earthquakes.

11:15-19 The 7th Trumpet
The mystery of God is accomplished (10:7).

| 11:15 | The verb used for 'has become' is past tense and speaks of something already accomplished. It refers to Christ's death and resurrection, not the second coming. Note the gospel statement again stimulates response of worship (v.17). |
| 11:19 | The ark of the covenant is visible. Indicates way to God's presence is open. |

What have we learnt?

1. Whatever happens, i.e. drought, famine, earthquake, etc. we must not be surprised and must remember that God is in control.

2. The church is being, and will be, persecuted right to the end.

3. The final judgment is delayed to allow all to hear the gospel and repent. How should we behave in the light of these things?

1. Where in this Bible passage do we see indicators of God's sovereignty? (7:1-8; 8:7-12; 9:13-19) Why is this a comfort?

2. How does 9:20-21 indicate God's mercy? How should this affect our behaviour? (Living godly lives, telling others about Jesus so that they have an opportunity to repent, etc.)

Food Taster   Cover some food stuff on a table, so the group cannot see them. Some should be sweet, such as honey, jam, chocolate, etc. and some sour, such as lemon juice, natural yoghurt, sour sweets, etc. Ask for 2 volunteers (with no food allergies) to act as tasters. Blindfold them and give them the foods to try. The remaining members could vote prior to each food as to whether or not the taster will identify it. Once all foods have been tasted, ask what 2 types of taste were represented to see if any can guess that they were sweet or sour. Today's Bible passage is about a message that John found sweet (good to hear) and sour (hard to take).

In small groups either produce a news article or T.V. news report based on chapters 8-9. Each group should choose a different incident to record. Give them 10-15 minutes to work on their project. If there is insufficient time to show the other groups what they have done, this could be done as a lead in activity next time.

PREPARATION

Revelation 12:1 - 14:20

LESSON AIMS

Satan's time is short. Christ has won the victory. You have to choose between God or Satan.

These chapters are at the centre of the book and tie the whole book together. They deal with 2 main themes, from the birth of Jesus until the outbreak of persecution against the Asian Christians (100 years), and the gospel. As you read them try and visualise what John is describing as this helps with understanding the overall message. In this episode there are no obvious signs as there were in the previous 2 episodes, (seals, trumpets). However, the episode is similar in that it can be divided into 6 scenes followed by an interlude. As in the previous episodes, the scenes are concurrent, not consecutive.

12:1-6   Scene 1 - the first coming of Jesus

12:1   The woman with the 12 stars on her head signifies the true Israel, (12 stars indicate 12 tribes). The fact that she is in heaven signifies her ultimate triumph.

12:2   The woman's suffering identifies her as Mary. We need to recognise that the same symbol can mean different things in different places (cf. v.6 where the woman becomes the Jerusalem church).

12:3   The dragon is Satan, (cf. 12:9, Genesis 3:1-19). The 7 heads and 10 horns symbolise his pretensions to divine wisdom and power (heads symbolise wisdom, horns symbolise power).

12:4   Note the limitation of the dragon's power - only a third of the stars were swept away (a third symbolises many, but not the majority). Here the dragon refers to Herod the Great and the massacre of the children (Matthew 2:16-18).

12:5   The male child is Jesus, cf. Psalm 2:9, (recognised by Jews to be a reference to the Messiah).

        'Snatched up' refers to the ascension.

12:6   The Jerusalem church fled to Pella beyond Jordan (the wilderness) at the outbreak of the Jewish revolt in AD 66. This church escaped the most hostile attentions of the Imperial power during the first century.

12:7-12   Scene 2 - Satan's defeat

12:7-9   There is war in heaven and the devil and all his angels are thrown out. This refers to the conquest of Satan at the cross (cf. v.11). Jesus has already won the victory through his death and resurrection.

12:10-12   Satan is furious at his defeat and turns his attention to the church (v.12). Although the devil is powerful his time is short-lived. The church will ultimately triumph over evil.

12:13 - 13:1   Scene 3 - Satan makes war on the church

12:13   In this scene the woman is the church of Jerusalem.

12:14   See the notes on v.6. Note the time mentioned (a time, times and half a time) - this refers to a period in history that is finite (see use of numbers in Series Overview and Week 16, 11:2).

12:15-16   John may have been referring to a flood and earthquake that took place at the time of the persecution of the Jerusalem church.

12:17   The rest of her offspring is the body of believers, the church.

13:1-10   Scene 4 - the beast from the sea

13:1   Jews thought the sea was where evil dwelt. Note that the beast has 7 heads and 10 horns like the dragon. The heads are crowned, symbolising preoccupation with sovereignty rather than wisdom. The horns indicate power. In John's day this beast symbolised Roman imperial power, but its description is true of totalitarian

regimes down the ages. This beast
- given power by Satan (v.2),
- has absolute authority (vv.4,7),
- causes men to worship Satan (v.4),
- persecutes the church (v.7),
- worshipped by all those who do
  not belong to God (v.8).

13:2 The description of the beast from the sea has similarities to the beasts of Daniel 7:4-6.

13:3 The beast has a fatal wound that has healed, counterfeiting the Lamb (5:6).

13:5 Note the time span - long, but limited.

13:10 Note the response required from the Christian. A far cry from the triumphalist gospel preached in some circles today.

13:11-18 **Scene 5 - the beast from the earth**

13:11-12 The pseudo-lamb speaks with Satan's voice and stands for state-dominated religion. In John's day this symbolised the High Priest of that part of Asia, who officiated at the Emperor worship that occurred at the annual meeting of all the cities in pro-consular Asia. The 2 horns show that this beast is weaker than the beast from the sea. In 16:13 and 19:20 this beast is identified as the false prophet. This beast
- supports the first beast and makes people worship it (v.12),
- is a worker of miracles (v.13),
- is a deceiver (v.14),
- is in control of all commerce (v.16-17).

The first beast stands for the anti-God state, the second for state-dominated religion.

13:16 The false prophet causes everyone to be marked, a comparison with the mark on the foreheads of the redeemed (7:3; 9:4).

13:18 6 is man's number. However many times repeated, it always falls short of God's number (7). No matter how powerful the beast is, it is not God. The false prophet may be inspired by Satan, but he is only human. 666 probably referred to Nero, who was the first great persecutor of Christians. In John's day many believed he would be brought back to life to continue persecution (cf. v.15).

14:1-5 **Scene 6 - in heaven**

14:1 Jesus stands with the multitude of the redeemed. Here the 144,000 refers to Jewish and Gentile believers. They are redeemed (v.3), not defiled with prostitution (v.4), followers of the Lamb (v.4, cf. Mark 8:34), and people of truth (v.5).

14:4 This is a difficult verse. It does not refer to those who have not married, as the Bible views marriage as God's way for people, (e.g. Genesis 2:20-24). In John's day cult worship involved prostitution with temple women, so it must refer to those who are faithful to God. The prophets frequently used this figurative language, e.g. idolatrous Israel as a prostitute or adulteress (Jeremiah 2:20, Hosea 1:2). The first fruits were the part of the harvest which belonged to God (Deuteronomy 26:1-11).

14:6-13 **Interlude**
As in previous episodes (see Week 16) the interlude is split into 2 parts.

14:6-11 **3 angels present the gospel**
No-one can sit on the fence - you either worship God and are saved, or the beast and are damned.

14:8 Babylon was a byword for pride and vainglory (see Genesis 11:1-9 for the original Babylon, the city of rebelliousness). In John's day Babylon was Rome. Every age has its Babylon - the personification of all the greed, luxury and pleasure that entice men away from God.

14:12-13 **A call to faithfulness**
Proclamation of the gospel always results in persecution of Christians. The response required from the Christian is patient endurance.

14:14-20 **Scene 7 - judgment**
The final judgment is symbolised by the harvest, cf. Joel 3:13, Matthew 13:41-42.

14:14 Cf. Daniel 7:13. This is a picture of Jesus coming as Judge. Jesus' first coming was to bring salvation, but his second coming is to bring judgment.

14:15 The angel with the message comes from the temple, signifying the message is from God the Father (cf. Mark 13:32).

14:17 Another angel gathers up what Jesus has harvested.

14:20 A stadion was about 202 yards. 1600 stadia is clearly another symbolical number - 4 (which stands for the earth) x 4 x 10 x 10 - the complete destruction of the wicked throughout the earth.

What have we learnt?

1. The Christian's struggle is against Satan - all oppression is Satanic in origin.
2. However powerful Satan appears, his time is short-lived and Christ has already triumphed over him at the cross.
3. The anti-God state and its state-dominated religion are forces to be reckoned with, but God will ultimately triumph.
4. The Christian is called to patiently endure persecution. (The above 3 points are the teaching by which Christians **can** endure.)
5. You cannot sit on the fence - you either worship God and are saved, or Satan and are damned.

1. Twice in these verses Christians are called to be faithful and endure patiently (13:5-10; 14:9-13). What have we learned from this passage to help us endure persecution?

2. Whom will you serve? Read 14:6-11. In these verses we are presented with two options for worship. What are they? Is it possible to serve both?

Dodge Ball   Divide the group into 2 teams. One team runs around inside a central, confined area and the other team has soft balls to throw at them, aiming to hit them below the knee. When a team member is hit he/she is out. Once all the team members are out, swap over roles. Record the length of time taken to get the whole team out. The team to do it in the shortest time wins. Today's Bible passage shows us that, like the game, we are on either one team or the other - God's or Satan's. We cannot be on both. Also, life as a Christian will not be easy; it will be hard, like trying to dodge the balls in the game. Let's see what reason the Bible gives us for taking heart when we are undergoing hard times. (Jesus has already won the victory.)

Photocopy page 62 for each group member. The word in the shaded column is 'triumphed'.

Using your Bible, answer the following questions and insert your answers in the grid. All the answers can be found in Revelation 14. When you have finished, the letters in the shaded column will spell the missing word from the statement below.

1. Where was the Lamb standing? (14:1, 2 words)

2. Where were the Lamb's and Father's names written? (14:1)

3. What implement was used for reaping? (14:15)

4. As what were the redeemed offered to God? (14:4)

5. How are the redeemed described in verse 5?

6. What was proclaimed? (14:6)

7. What are the saints commanded to remain to Jesus? (14:12)

8. From where did the voice speak? (14:13)

9. How are the dead, who die in the Lord, described? (14:13)

Jesus .... over Satan at the cross.

How does this statement help Christians endure persecution?

PREPARATION

Revelation

15:1 - 16:21

LESSON AIMS

To understand that when God comes in judgment it will be too late to repent.

These chapters deal with the final judgment and end of the physical world. The destruction here is total, not partial as in chapters 8-9. This must happen before a new world can be formed.

15:1-8   **Prelude to the end of the world**

15:1   Tells us that what is to come is the final judgment (7 last plagues).

15:2   The fire mixed in the sea speaks of judgment (cf. 20:14).

In John's day the beast symbolised the cult of Emperor worship. The image symbolised the statues set up for worship of the Emperor, and the number of his name symbolised his real identity, i.e. man pretending to be God.

15:3   Cf. Exodus 15 - a song of deliverance. Moses was the leader of the Old Covenant, the Lamb is the leader of the New.

15:5-6   The angels came out of the temple, indicating that the coming trials are the righteous judgments of God.

16:1-12   **The first 6 plagues**

16:2-9   The first 4 plagues affect the physical environment (cf. the first 4 trumpets, 8:7-12). Note their similarity to some of the plagues in Egypt (Exodus 5-10).

16:9   Note the reaction to the 5th plague - men still refused to repent.

16:10-12   The 5th and 6th plagues affect mankind. The 6th plague is the destruction of mankind by the kings of the whole world (global warfare). In John's day, the River Euphrates was the border of civilisation and people were fearful of the kings living to the east of it.

16:13-16   **Interlude**

16:13-14   The miraculous signs convince the kings of the whole world that they can vanquish God's people.

16:15   This verse is a reassurance for the Christians that they have nothing to fear on that day when mankind is destroyed (cf. Matthew 24:42-44).

16:16   Armageddon - the hill fortress of Megiddo was the scene of so many battles that it came to stand for battle itself. This is the only mention of Armageddon in Scripture.

16:17-21   **The 7th plague**
The destruction of the air, resulting in the final destruction of the world.

16:19   Civilisation is destroyed, including all the cities and monuments built by rebel people. This verse shows very clearly that there is no future for the Christian in the old order (Babylon) and there will never be a utopia on the old earth.

16:20   The world will be destroyed at the word of God (v.17) just as it was created by that word (Genesis 1).

QUESTIONS

1. God is holy. In the light of this how should we approach him?

2. God gives everyone an opportunity to repent (16:9,11). Am I able to explain the gospel of Jesus Christ to my friends?

3. There is no future for the Christian in the old order (Babylon), and there will never be a utopia on our present earth. How should this knowledge affect our priorities? (NB The command given to Adam in Genesis 1:26-28 still pertains in this limited temporal environment, so 'Don't bother with it!' is not an option).

FOCUS ACTIVITY

Too Late! Ask one person from the group to leave the room, telling them that they can return whenever they like. Set a task for the remaining people in the room, such as stacking the chairs, creating a human pyramid, or whatever, which they must try to complete before the person outside the room returns. Offer a significant reward to the group if they complete the task. Of course if the person returns before they have completed the task then they are TOO LATE and no matter how well they have done or how far they have got they do not get the reward.

This activity introduces the concept of being too late. Today we will look at what it means to be too late when God comes in judgment.

ACTIVITY

Photocopy page 65 for each group member.

The shaded letters spell 'marvellous' (15:3).

Starting with the longest word, enter every word of the Bible verse below into the crossword grid. Underline each word as you position it. When you have finished the letters in the shaded squares will spell a word that describes God's deeds.

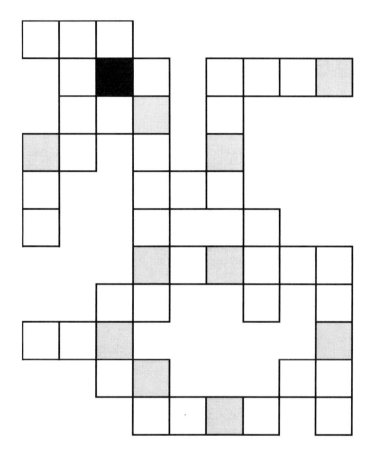

All men will hate you because of me, but he who stands firm to the end will be saved.

Mark 13:13

God's deeds are great and ……………………………..

Which verse is this from?   Revelation 15:

PREPARATION

Revelation 17:1 - 19:21

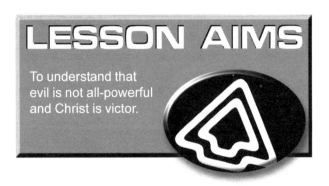

LESSON AIMS

To understand that evil is not all-powerful and Christ is victor.

The next 2 studies look at the end of evil. This study deals with the destruction of the beast (the empire) and the false prophet (the anti-Christ), and next week looks at the destruction of the dragon (Satan).

17:1-18   The woman and the beast

17:1   In John's day the 'great prostitute' was Rome (v.18). In our day it is any human system organised independently of God and so in rebellion against the Creator.

'Many waters' - see 17:15 for the interpretation. The literal Babylon was built on many waters (Jeremiah 51:13).

17:2   'Committed adultery' - joined to, by means of political and economic treaties.

17:3   The beast is the beast from the sea (13:1ff. - see week 17). Scarlet speaks of ostentatious splendour and indicates imperial and regal status. The beast refers to the Emperor. The blasphemous names signify the cult of Emperor worship. The picture is of the empire riding on the back of the Emperor.

The 10 horns are identified as 10 kings who have limited authority (v.12), and probably stood for the 10 provincial governors in that part of Asia. The governors served for 1 year.

The 7 heads are identified as 7 hills (v.9) and also 7 kings. They are presumed to refer to the different Emperors - 5 have already been, 1 is now and 1 is to come (v.10). The 8th beast probably refers to Domitian (AD 81-96), who was thought by many to be a reincarnation of Nero, the great persecutor of the church (v.11).

17:4   Cf. Jeremiah 51:7.

17:5   Roman harlots wore their names on their foreheads. 'Mystery' probably indicates

that the name is not to be taken literally but symbolically.

17:7   In apocalyptic literature revelations are made in symbols, which remain mysteries until the appropriate interpretation is supplied (cf. Daniel 2:18-19; 5:5-12; 7:15ff.).

17:8   The Beast - cf. 11:7; 13:3-8.

'Once was, now is not' - at times evil powers rampage through history, at times they go underground, but they always return. This is a parody of the true ruler, the Lamb. Jesus once was incarnate, now has ascended (is not), and will one day return in glory to judge the living and the dead. The beast came from the Abyss (the dominion of Satan) and will be destroyed(v.11).

17:9   Rome was a city set on 7 hills and was then the centre of the civilised world. (As there are other cities set on 7 hills, such as Bath, the woman should not be identified as referring to a specific city for all time.)

17:11   'Goes to destruction' - cf. 2 Thessalonians 2:3-4.

17:14   God will overcome. See 19:11-21 for details.

17:15   All nations were ruled by Rome.

17:16-18   In the end the leaders of the empire turn on the Emperor and destroy him. Rome falls from within, which has been true of most major civilisations.

18:1-24   **The destruction of Babylon**
Chapter 18 describes the sure collapse of all human organisations, commercial or otherwise, that leave God out of their reckoning. It echoes the spirit and language of all the great 'downfall'

prophecies in the OT, (Isaiah 13 - 14; 24, Jeremiah 50 - 51, Ezekiel 26 - 28). It is one final, comprehensive judgment on every power in every age that has grown fat on evil and treats men as mere commodities to be bought and sold (v.13).

For 'Babylon' see notes in Week 17, 14:8. The judgment of Babylon was first announced in 14:8, then again in 16:19.

18:4   God's people are tempted to come to terms with the world, but must not.

18:8   However the destruction of 'Babylon' occurs, it is due to the judgment of God. This great city of rebel people will be replaced by the New Jerusalem (21:2).

19:1-8   **God's people rejoice**

19:1-2   The gospel is proclaimed, followed by worship (v.6-7). See notes on 7:10-12 (Week 16). Judgment is directed at civilisations and rulers, not just at individual men and women.

19:6   The keynote of the book, our Lord God Almighty reigns!

19:7-8   In contrast to the destruction of the prostitute, the people of God rejoice at the readiness of the bride.

19:9-10   **Prophecy**
These words of prophecy are given as comfort to the people of God. They are the truly blessed ones, even though, in the eyes of the world, they appear weak and forsaken.

19:11-21   **The destruction of the beast and the anti-Christ (false prophet)**
This passage is yet another indication that what John is giving us are not literal pictures. Jesus comes on a horse, with a sword coming out of his mouth, and the birds of heaven are summoned to eat the flesh of his foes, whom he shall overthrow. This is a vivid picture of a complete victory, but is obviously not a literal one. We are told twice over that the implement of victory is a sword proceeding from the mouth of the conqueror (vv.15,21). God needs only to speak and his enemies are defeated.

19:15   Cf. Hebrews 4:12-13.

'Rod of iron' - see Psalm 2:9.

19:19-20   The beast and false prophet do not realise that the battle has been won already at the cross. Note the anti-climax - there is no final battle. The beast and false prophet are captured and thrown into the lake of fire.

NB Christ conquers using the power of the gospel - it was the way he conquered when he was tempted, the way he has conquered down the ages, and the way he will conquer at the end. The cross and the empty tomb are the ultimate place of conquest.

What have we learnt?

1.   The battle against Satan and the powers of evil has already been won at the cross, regardless of appearances to the contrary.

2.   The Christian is truly blessed of God, even when undergoing persecution.

3.   The Christian must resist coming to terms with the world and taking on the world's values.

4.   The gospel is powerful. We need to know it and proclaim it.

QUESTIONS

1. When we look at our culture, the Christian church appears to be small and insignificant. How does what we have learnt help us to persevere as Christians?

2. What practical steps can we take as a group to avoid taking on the world's values?

FOCUS ACTIVITY

All Powerful Organise a simple competition amongst the group members, such as arm wrestling or 'Back to Back' wrestling.

Arm Wrestling: competitors face each other, interlock hands and try to push the other person's hand back down onto the table.

Back to Back Wrestling: competitors sit back to back on the floor and interlock their arms behind themselves. The object is to pull your opponent to the right until they topple over onto their side.

Obviously, the winner is the person who beats the most people. This introduces the idea of someone being all-powerful. Ideally, it would be great if there was someone in the group who beat everybody, but even if there is not, it still introduces the theme. Today we will see what is not all-powerful, as well as who is.

ACTIVITY

Photocopy page 69 for each group member. The sentence remaining in the grid is 'Jesus has already won the victory.'

Find the following words from today's Bible passage in the word square. Each word reads backwards or forwards in a straight line horizontally, vertically or diagonally. No letter is used more than once.

ALMIGHTY	JUSTICE	SALVATION	WISDOM
AUTHORITY	KINGDOM	SCEPTRE	WORSHIPPED
FAITHFUL	LAMB	SWORD	
GLORY	POWER	THRONE	
HALLELUJAH	PRAISE	TRUE	

M	O	D	S	I	W	J	Y	T	R	U	E
T	H	R	O	N	E	T	E	J	S	L	W
D	U	H	S	G	H	H	U	A	M	U	O
R	N	S	A	G	L	S	A	O	P	F	R
O	L	O	I	L	T	O	D	R	R	H	S
W	E	M	I	I	L	G	R	P	A	T	H
S	L	A	C	T	N	E	O	Y	I	I	I
A	D	E	Y	I	A	W	L	W	S	A	P
O	N	T	K	H	E	V	E	U	E	F	P
L	A	M	B	R	V	I	L	C	J	T	E
E	R	T	P	E	C	S	O	A	R	A	D
A	U	T	H	O	R	I	T	Y	S	Y	H

Now, starting from the top and reading from left to right, write down the remaining letters in the blanks below to discover something that helps us to persevere as Christians.

_ _ _ _   _ _ _   _ _ _ _ _ _ _   _ _ _   _ _ _   _ _ _ _ _ _ _ .

PREPARATION

Revelation 20:1-15

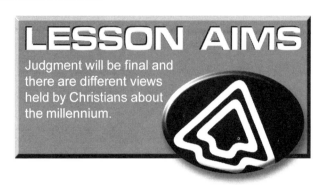

LESSON AIMS

Judgment will be final and there are different views held by Christians about the millennium.

The Millennium

In looking at the concept of the millennium, we need to be clear about the principles underlying Scripture interpretation. Precise and clear Scripture must be our guide in the interpretation of the figurative and obscure. We must not take a doctrine from an obscure passage and impose it on the rest of Scripture. There is no mention of a 1,000 year reign of Christ on earth anywhere else in the NT. The word millennium does not occur elsewhere and the concept is unknown outside Revelation 20. Even where Paul expressly deals with the Jews and their future (Romans 11) he does not mention national restoration and Jewish pre-eminence under an earthly Messianic rule. The Gospels, Acts and Epistles teach that Jesus' second coming accompanies the general resurrection and final judgment of all. We noted this in Revelation (10:7; 11:15-18) and will see it again in 20:11-15. Before looking at Revelation 20 the following terms need to be clearly understood:

1. Post-millennialism

This states that the second coming of Christ will follow the millennium (1000 year reign of the faithful on earth). The kingdom of Christ is now in existence and will gradually extend its borders through the preaching of the gospel. At the end there will be 1,000 years when Christianity will prevail throughout the world. Evil will be restrained and Satan bound. This is followed by an outbreak of evil and a terrible final battle with Satan's forces (Armageddon), after which Christ will come again and the dead will be raised and judged.

Problems with this view:
a) The Bible does not teach the prospect of a converted world before Christ comes again (see Matthew 13:24-30, where wheat and tares will grow together).

b) It is strange that, at the end of 1,000 years of righteousness, Satan will lead a host to battle from the 4 quarters of the earth and surround a city of God's people, who are only saved by supernatural means (20:7-9). From

where is this host to come if righteousness prevails in a converted world (Luke 18:8, 2 Thessalonians 2:1-12)?

2. Pre-millennialism

This states that the second coming of Christ introduces the millennium. The commonly held order of events is as follows:

a) A period of apostasy preceding Christ's coming.

b) Christ comes in secret and raises the dead in Christ, snatching them away with the living believers (the secret rapture). Based on Matthew 24:36-41.

c) A 7 year period of great tribulation when the anti-Christ rules the earth (Daniel 9:25-27; 12:9-13).

d) Jesus comes openly. Armageddon is fought and the anti-Christ defeated. Jesus reigns in Jerusalem for 1,000 years and the temple and sacrificial worship are restored. (Zechariah 8:1-9; 12:1 - 14:21).

e) At the end of 1,000 years Satan is loosed again and stirs up rebellion against God. He is defeated. This is followed by the resurrection of the wicked and their judgment. Some pre-millennialists miss out stage b (the secret rapture).

Problems with this view:
a) Jesus taught that the resurrection of his people would be on 'the last day' (John 5:39-40; 11:24) - that same 'last day' when judgment would come upon the wicked (John 12:47-48).

b) See problem b under post-millennialism.

c) There is no teaching in Scripture to back up the idea of 1,000 years when all the blessings of Christ's kingdom are shared by thousands of Christ-rejecting people who have survived the great tribulation and Christ's second coming.

3. A(non)-millennialism

This states that the concept of 1,000 years of earthly blessedness is a wrong interpretation of Revelation 20:1-6. The order of events is as follows:

a) Christ's second coming will be preceded by widespread apostasy which will culminate in the appearance of the anti-Christ.

b) This final rebellion against Christ will be overthrown by him at his second coming, when he will take to himself the true believers, both living and dead.

c) At the same time the wicked dead will also be raised for judgment. The earth and its works will be destroyed (2 Peter 3:7-10). A new heaven and new earth will appear in which only righteousness dwells.

In *Apocalypse Now and Then*, Paul Barnett suggests that the number 1,000 is a symbolic one, just like all the other numbers in Revelation, and indicates a very long time. The millennium begins with the first resurrection (20:5) and ends with the second death (20:6). The first resurrection is Christ's historic resurrection, by virtue of which all believers are raised, and the second death is when Christ comes in judgment and the dragon (Satan) is thrown into the lake of fire (20:14). Therefore the millennium refers to the whole of the period of history between Christ's resurrection and his second coming.

All 3 views have been, and are, held by godly men and women. Let us look at what the passage says, leaving aside preconceived ideas.

20:1-10 **The defeat of Satan**
Chapter 19 shows us God's victory over the prime agents of Satan, the beast and the false prophet. It does not give details of the victory over Satan; these are given in 20:1-10.

20:1-3 Satan is bound - he is under God's firm control. The NT teaches that Satan's power was defeated on the cross, e.g. Colossians 2:13-15, Hebrews 2:14, John 12:31. Jesus teaches about the 'strong man' being bound in Matthew 12:25-29. In 2 Peter 2:4 we see the angels who sinned (including Satan) cast down into hell to await judgment, but 1 Peter 5:8 speaks of Satan as still being active. Satan being active, but under restraint, is shown clearly in Job 1:6-12; 2:1-6.

This is also consistent with the teaching of Revelation. In 9:1 Satan was given the key to the Abyss, it was not his by right. In 12:13-17 his war on the woman and her seed (the church) was unsuccessful.

20:2 1,000 years speaks of God's complete authority over Satan. It is not a literal interpretation. See introductory notes. Satan is defeated by Christ's death.

20:3 The reason for the restricted binding of Satan is that he should not deceive the nations. Some think this means that Satan is unable to curtail the spread of the gospel throughout the world. See notes on v.8 regarding the deceit of the nations.

20:4-6 These verses show us what is happening in heaven during this same period.

20:4 Elsewhere in Revelation, thrones are in heaven (e.g. 4:4). The use of the words 'thrones' and 'souls' indicates heaven, not earth.

The company described are those who, throughout the ages, have died because of their witness to Christ and refusal to worship the beast (13:11-17).

'Risen with Christ' is used in the NT to speak of the state of the true believer, e.g. Colossians 3:1, Ephesians 2:6, Romans 6:5-8.

20:5 The first resurrection is Jesus' resurrection. The dead in Christ have gone to heaven and reign with him because of his resurrection. The other dead wait for the second resurrection. The 1,000 years is the time between the first resurrection on Easter Sunday and Jesus' second coming (the second resurrection).

20:7-10 Satan incites world rebellion and is defeated by supernatural means. There will be a short period of intense persecution before Satan is finally overthrown.

20:8 Gog and Magog (see Ezekiel 38) are a symbol of the world powers opposed to God. Satan's deceit of the nations was to gather them for battle against God's people. This verse talks about the same events as 16:14-16 and 19:19, John just repeats things in a different form. Satan is overthrown at the same time as the beast and the false prophet.

20:9 The camp is the community of God's people and is in contrast to the great city of Babylon (18:10), because it is not their permanent home.

20:10 Cf. Matthew 25:41. The beast and false prophet stand for systems rather than individuals, so this speaks of the total and permanent destruction of evil.

20:11-15 The second death

20:11   See Daniel 7:9-10, Revelation 1:13-16, John 5:27, Matthew 25:31-32.

Earth and sky fled away, cf. Isaiah 34:2-4, 2 Peter 3:10. The whole natural order is destroyed prior to the creation of the new heaven and earth (21:1).

20:12   This speaks of a general judgment. All the dead are there, including those whose names are written in the book of life. Salvation is always by grace (Ephesians 2:8-9); divine judgement is always according to works (Revelation 2:23; 22:12, Romans 2:6).

20:13   Death at sea was especially abhorred in those days as there was nowhere to place a memorial.

20:14   See 1 Corinthians 15:26.

The second death is so called because it befell those who were raised from the first death (Hebrews 9:27).

NB The specifics given are not intended to satisfy curiosity about the eschatological details, but to remind us of how we should live in the light of a definite final judgment (2 Peter 3:11-18).

What have we learnt?

1. Satan is limited in what he can achieve. He was defeated at the cross.

2. When judgment comes it will be final. How does this affect the way we live?

3. There are different views about the millennium (1,000 years) and all are held by godly people. It should never become a reason for division, as it is not to do with the only way of salvation being through Jesus' death on the cross.

1. When we look at the suffering in our world, whatever its cause, how does what we have learnt help us to persevere in the Christian life?

2. What difference does the knowledge that God's judgment will be final make to our lives?

Here Comes the Judge   Set up 3-4 judging areas, such as you would find in a local show/fete. Suggestions are: the best potato (or other vegetable), the best flower, the best footballer, the best pop singer, etc. Give each person a piece of paper and a pen and ask them to judge the exhibits without reference to other members of the group. When they have finished ask them to feed back which item in each category they have judged to be the best and why. Discuss the criteria they used for judging - looks, smell, size, sound, etc. Ask if they were to repeat the exercise in a year's time, would they judge in the same way? If not, why not? Today we will look at how God judges and see how it differs from the way we do. (See 1 Samuel 16:7.)

Photocopy page 73 for each group member.

The letter groups remaining in the grid spell 'Judgment is final'.

To discover an important fact, answer the following questions from today's Bible passage. The answers have been broken into groups of letters which can be found in the grid. The numbers in brackets refer to the number of letters in the answer. As you answer each question cross off the relevant letters.

LPH	ENT	KO	JUD	HA	ON
GME	THA	NIN	EDE	SE	IFE
FL	ES	DES	THR	BOO	NTI
RP	AD	SFI	DEA	WH	GSU
BUR	ITE	ND	UR	NAL	TH

1. What term used for Satan in verse 2 reminds us of Genesis 3? (7)
2. Where were those with authority to judge seated? (7)
3. Satan was thrown into the lake of .... (7, 7)
4. What colour was the throne in verse 11? (5)
5. Who stood before the throne? (3, 4)
6. What other book was opened in verse 12? (4, 2, 4)
7. What else was thrown into the fire in verse 14? (5, 3, 5)

Now write the remaining groups of letters in order to discover something important.

_ _ _ _ _ _ _ _   _ _   _ _ _ _ _.

How should this knowledge affect the way we live?

PREPARATION
Revelation 21:1 - 22:21

LESSON AIMS
It will be wonderful to be forever with Jesus. We should live in the light of his imminent return.

21:1 - 22:5 The New Creation

These verses contain a wonderful description of what it will be like in heaven, with nothing to mar a perfect relationship with God.

21:1-4 New heaven and new earth

21:1 It all takes pace after the judgment and dissolution of the present world (see Isaiah 65:17-19, 2 Peter 3:13).

The sea symbolised separation to the Jew. In 13:1 it casts up the system that is hostile to God and his people. It was the place where evil dwelt.

21:2 The new Jerusalem is the bride (the church), cf. Galatians 4:26, Ephesians 5:25-27, Hebrews 11:10; 12:22. It is the community of believers and is contrasted with the city of Babylon, the community of unbelievers (17:5). One community worships the Lamb and is on its way to heaven, the other worships the beast and is on its way to hell (the fiery lake).

21:3 The voice from the throne is God. Following the rescue from Egypt God symbolically dwelt among his people in the tabernacle. Now he lives with them in reality. This is the final rescue.

21:4 There will be no more suffering for a Christian.

21:5-8 Challenge to evangelism

21:5 God announces his plan to make a new creation (v.1-4). God's statement is reliable (trustworthy and true) and it will definitely come to pass (v.6).

Trustworthy and true are titles applied to Jesus (3:14, 19:11).

21:6 Cf. John 7:37; 4:13-14. God's name signifies his reliability. He is the great I AM (Exodus 3:14-15).

21:8 Paul Barnett, in *Apocalypse Now and Then* (p.155), suggests this verse is dealing with 2 categories of people. There are the lapsed Christians (cowardly, unbelieving, vile) and those who have always worshipped the beast (murderers, sexually immoral, magicians, idolaters, liars). This is difficult to equate with John 10:25-30, where Jesus states clearly that those who are his will never be snatched away. At the final judgment all will be made plain and there may well be those who have appeared to be Christian but have never truly belonged to the Lord Jesus.

These verses are a grim reminder of the fate of the unbeliever and an encouragement to Christians to persevere until the end. It is also a reason for evangelism.

21:9-21 The holy city

21:11 The new city is beautiful (cf. the first creation, Genesis 1:31). See also vv.19-21.

21:12-14 The true Israel is the new Israel, the faithful from both dispensations, based on God's redemptive acts from both the old and new covenants. Note the repeated use of 12 in the description (see Introductory notes).

21:16 12,000 stadia is approximately the same distance as from London to Athens, the same as the then known world. It is not meant literally, but is a picture of the immensity of the city. On earth God's people may seem few and scattered, but they are part of a vast heavenly city.

The city was a perfect cube, like the Most Holy Place in the temple (1 Kings 6:20). Here the whole city is a cube, the place where God dwells, so there is no need of a special sanctuary.

| 21:19-20 | The list of jewels echoes those which were set in the High Priest's breastplate to represent Israel (Exodus 28:15-21). |

21:22 - 22:5 Worship in the holy city

21:22	In the new Jerusalem every believer can approach God without going to a special place (the temple) or going through a special person (priest).
21:24	The people who live in the city include the Gentiles (the nations and the kings of the earth), cf. Genesis 22:18, Galatians 3:8.
22:1	See Ezekiel 47:1-12, Zechariah 14:8.
22:2	Fallen man was denied access to the tree of life (Genesis 3:22-24). Now the edict is reversed.
22:4	Cf. 13:16.

22:6-21 Epilogue

22:11	Once Christ comes, each individual will be fixed in their attitudes and it will be too late to change. We should live in the light of the imminent return of Christ (2 Peter 3:10-14).
22:13	Cf. 1:8; 21:6.
22:15	Cf. 21:8.
22:16	Cf. 5:5; 2:28, 2 Peter 1:19.
22:18-19	John gives warnings against tampering with what he has written.

What have we learnt?

1. Heaven is a wonderful place!
2. There are only 2 communities and each person has to choose where they stand -

   worshipping Christ or the beast,

   belonging to the new Jerusalem or Babylon,

   on their way to heaven or hell.
3. We need to tell people about Jesus so that they can be saved.
4. We should live in the light of the imminent return of Christ.

1. Go round the group asking them to state one thing they have learnt through studying Revelation.

2. In the light of 21:1-4, should Christians expect to have problem-free lives?

3. There are only 2 communities - which one do you belong to? Can you sit on the fence?

Happiness is ... Divide the group into pairs and ask them to describe to each other the happiest experience they have ever had, or the thing that would most make them happy. If you have time you could get people to feed back to the whole group.

This introduces the theme of joy and happiness, which will pale into insignificance compared with heaven. Let's see how the Bible describes heaven.

A quiz. Divide the group into 2 teams.

The winner is the first team to collect 6 precious stones (see diagram). Label 12 of the stones with the names of those decorating the foundations of the city in Revelation 21:19-20. Leave the remaining 4 stones blank.

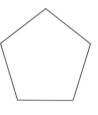

Requirements

Each team requires a set of 8 precious stones, 6 labelled and 2 blank. Each team's stones are randomly numbered from 1-8 on the back and are pinned to the board with the numbers showing. The blank stones introduce an element of chance so that a team member who answers a question incorrectly will not place their team in an irretrievable position. Prepare 16 questions to bring out the main points from the Bible passage.

Rules

A question is put to each team in turn and, if answered correctly, one of the team members chooses a stone by calling out its number. The stone is turned over and, if labelled, is left on the board. A blank stone is removed from the board. If an incorrect answer is given the question is offered to the other team.

Allow 10 minutes for the quiz.

PREPARATION

See lesson notes

LESSON AIMS

To understand the Bible's teaching on homosexuality.

Homosexuality is portrayed positively in schools, the media and some Christian circles. Our young people are being bombarded constantly with sexual images, many of which are homosexual. (See examples in television and magazine advertisements, explicit homosexual behaviour in soap operas, chat shows, etc.) It is no wonder that many of them are confused and unsure about what they should believe. At an increasingly young age children are being labelled 'gay' by their peers in the playground, because they enjoy close, same-sex friendships. They are under pressure to be 'politically correct' and often believe that taking a stance against homosexuality is being homophobic.

Contrary to popular opinion, homosexuality is not normal. If it were, the human race would have died out centuries ago. However, in many cultures today it is portrayed, often aggressively, as an equally valid lifestyle as heterosexuality. This does not mean that it is a valid lifestyle choice for a Christian, so our young people need to understand what the Bible teaches about it.

There is no specific Bible teaching about the homosexual condition, but there is explicit condemnation of homosexual acts in both the Old and New Testaments. We need to look carefully at what the Bible teaches and not try to make it mean either more or less than it says.

We are all human, made in the image of God. We are more than just sexual beings and to make our sexuality the most important part of us is to demean us as human beings. It is very easy to make sex into an idol and worship it rather than our Creator.

As with all the apologetics lessons, the information in these notes is to be assimilated by the teacher, who can then decide on an appropriate presentation to the group.

Introduction

Use the Focus Activity to introduce the concept of bias.

Define prejudice - a preconceived opinion or bias against (or in favour of) a person or thing.

Everyone has their prejudices.

Sometimes Christians are labelled as prejudiced because they say that homosexuality is a sin. (You might want to ask the group whether or not they think it is a sin.) There is a difference between sin and crime. The fact that something is socially legal does not make it acceptable to God, e.g. rape is both a crime and a sin, whereas adultery is not a crime, but is a sin. There is a difference between homosexual orientation (what a person is) and homosexual practice (what a person does). We may not have any control over our orientation, but we are all responsible for actions, whether hetero- or homosexual.

What does the OT say about homosexuality?

Genesis

19:1-25   God's judgment on Sodom and Gomorrah. Paraphrase the story, then ask the group to study verses 4-8 to see what was the sin of Sodom.

19:4-8   The men of Sodom wanted Lot's 2 visitors for sexual purposes (to know them), as is made clear by Lot offering his daughters in their place.

19:13   God was about to execute judgment on Sodom because of the people's sinfulness. God had told Abraham that he would go down to Sodom to see if they were as sinful as reported (18:20-21). God destroyed Sodom following the incident in 19:4-9, therefore the implication is that Sodom's sin was homosexuality.

Judges

19:13-26   This story is similar to Genesis 19 in that the men of Gibeah surround a house containing a visitor and demand that the visitor is given to them for sexual purposes (v.22). The visitor's concubine is given to the men instead (v.23-26). You might not want to use this passage as well as the Genesis one. If you do, approach it in the same way as the Genesis passage.

1 Kings

14:24   Homosexual prostitution was part of idolatrous worship.

Leviticus

18:22   Homosexual practice Is forbidden, along with incest (v.7-10), adultery (v.20) and bestiality (v.23). Note the link with idolatry (v.21).

It can be argued that the Genesis and Judges passages teach about God's condemnation of homosexual rape and have nothing to do with consensual homosexual practice within the bounds of a caring relationship. Equally, the passages in 1 Kings and Leviticus could be said to deal with homosexuality as an outworking of idolatry. Does this mean that the stance advocated by the Christian Gay and Lesbian Movement, that homosexual practice within the bounds of a caring relationship is acceptable to God, is correct?

What does the NT say about homosexuality?

Romans

1:22-27   These verses link homosexual practice with idolatry (v.23-24). However, Paul goes on to link both homosexuality and idolatry to sinful people departing from the Creator's purpose for them (v.25).

This implies that every homosexual act is sinful, regardless of sexual orientation, because it is contrary to God's creation plan for human sexual behaviour. Jesus never talks about homosexuality, but does give clear teaching on marriage.

Matthew

19:3-6   Jesus endorses the traditional Jewish teaching on God's plan for marriage (see Genesis 2:20-25), i.e. that it is lifelong, heterosexual and monogamous. This means that adultery, fornication, polygamy, polyandry and homosexual acts are **all** sins.

1 Corinthians

6:9-10   Homosexuals, along with the sexually immoral, idolaters and adulterers, will not be part of God's kingdom. However, note v.11 - 'such were some of you'. God's grace is such that his kingdom is open to all who repent and trust Jesus for salvation. Homosexuality is not the unforgivable sin.

1 Timothy

1:8-11   Another list of sinful practices. Note the similarity in v.9-10 with some of the Ten Commandments - honour father and mother, do not murder, do not commit adultery, do not bear false witness. Sexual immorality, homosexuality and adultery cover all sexual intercourse outside heterosexual marriage.

Ephesians

5:31-32   Marriage is used to symbolise Christ's relationship with his church (see also Revelation 21:1-2). All sexual sin gives a wrong model, not only of human relationships, but also of God's relationship with his people.

From the above passages it is clear that homosexual intercourse is a sin, but we are all human, sexual and sinners. Therefore, there is no place for feelings of moral superiority.

The 2 following passages indicate God's view of hypocrisy and pride.

Matthew

23:27-28   These verses are part of Jesus' declaration about the hypocrisy of the Scribes and Pharisees (the religious leaders). Jesus denounces their setting themselves up as righteous when they harbour sin in their hearts.

24:49-51   These verses come at the end of a section of teaching on being ready for the coming of the Son of Man in judgment. Note that the wicked servant will be put with the hypocrites in hell.

2 Timothy

3:1-5   Paul includes the proud in the list of the godless.

Implications

1.   We are all fallen human beings and we all sin.

2.   Everyone is a mix of complex desires. The important thing is what we do about them.

3.   We are saved by God's grace, not as a result of cleaning up our lives. As forgiven sinners, we need forgiveness daily.

4.   Contrary to our cultural expectations, we do not need to be in a sexual relationship (either hetero or homo) to be 'normal' or 'fulfilled'.

5.   The only alternative to heterosexual marriage is sexual abstinence.

6.   We should aim for godliness, not re-orientation.

7.   Sexual labels are unhelpful in that they can make sexuality into an idol. People are demeaned by making their sexuality the most important point. What matters is whether or not a person is in Christ.

QUESTIONS

1. As a group, how can we promote healthy relationships, both same-sex and between-sex?

2. Christians are called to accept God's standards and live by them. We all need God's grace to do this. What practical steps can we take to encourage and support each other in keeping to sexual abstinence outside marriage? (Consider social activities, contact outside church activities, e.g. by phone, praying for one another, etc., as well as avoiding situations where we might be tempted, unsuitable magazines, internet chat rooms, etc.)

3. Would someone with a homosexual orientation feel comfortable in our group?

FOCUS ACTIVITY

Beat the Bias Divide the group into teams and give each team a lemon and a pencil. (The lemons should not be too round.) Mark out a course and stand half of each team at one end of the course and half at the other end. On the command to start, a member of each team uses the pencil to push the lemon the length of the course. When they reach the other end they hand the pencil to the next team member, who pushes the lemon back to the start. Continue until all team members have had a go. The winning team is the first one to complete the task.

Comment on how difficult it was to push the lemon in a straight line, because the shape of the lemon gave it a bias.

OVERVIEW
The Dark Days of the Judges

SERIES AIMS

1. To understand the dangers of disobedience.
2. To understand more of the mercy and patience of God.

MEMORY WORK

For God will bring every deed into judgment, including every hidden thing, whether it is good or evil.

Ecclesiastes 12:14

The Dark Days of the Judges

The period of the Judges lasted for about 340 years from the death of Joshua until the establishment of the monarchy. During this time God raised up a succession of leaders (judges) to accomplish a specific purpose, i.e. deliverance / rescue. The same pattern of events can be seen with each judge:-

1. A period of disobedience by the Israelites.
2. Punishment through foreign oppression.
3. Repentance.
4. The raising up of judge or deliverer.

These judges were more than arbiters between the people. They were also the civil and military leaders of the Israelites. The choice of the judge was in God's hands; there was no dynastic succession.

Judge	Years as Judge	Enemies
Othniel	40	Mesopotmia (Aram)
Ehud	80	Moab
Shamgar	?	Philistines
Deborah (Barak)	40	Jabin of Canaan
Gideon	40	Midian
*Abimelech	3	Civil War
Tola	23	-
Jair	22	-
Jephthah	6	Ammon
Ibzan	7	-
Elon	10	-
Abdon	8	-
Samson	20	Philistines
Samuel	?	Phlistines

* Some commentators do not list Abimelech as a judge because he was self appointed, not God's choice.

The book of Judges shows the results of continual disobedience of God. The Israelites no longer had peace, prosperity and victory over their enemies (as seen in the book of Joshua). Their disobedience was shown in many ways:-

1. failure to occupy and purge the land (1:27-36)

2. Baal worship (2:11-13)

3. intermarriage (3:5-6)

4. pagan influence (3:5-6)

5. making of images (17:1-4)

6. establishment of private sanctuaries (17:5-6, cf. Deuteronomy 12:2-5)

7. improper pride (17:1-4)

8. stealing (18:14-20)

9. sexual sin (19:1-30)

10. standing up for the guilty (20:12-16)

11. low respect for human life (21:8-14)

12. violation of personal rights (21:19-22)

The book can be summed up by 21:25, 'In those days Israel had no king; everyone did as he saw fit'. But in spite of all this, God was merciful and ready to save his people when they turned to him in repentance and faith.

This series looks at 3 of the major judges, Ehud, Deborah and Jephthah, and at Abimelech, the self-appointed judge. The first lesson deals with the background to the book and introduces the cyclic nature of events - Israel's sad-go-round. The remaining 4 lessons show the deterioration of events as Israel becomes more entangled with her pagan neighbours.

PREPARATION

Judges 2:6-23

LESSON AIMS

To understand the cyclic pattern of the book of Judges.

2:6	'Take possession of the land' - the Israelites did this only partially, cf. 1:27-36, and the consequence of this was seen in further compromise and the recurring pattern of sin.
2:8	'Servant of the Lord' - i.e. his official representative, as was Moses (Exodus 14:31). In the New Testament all Christians are called servants.
2:10	'Gathered to their fathers' - a description of death, cf. Genesis 25:7.
2:10-15	The apostasy of the Israelites - they did evil, served Baal, forsook the Lord and followed and worshipped the gods of the people around. God's reaction was anger; he handed them over, sold them, his hand was against them and they were in great distress.
2:13	Baal meant 'Lord'. Baal, the god worshipped by the Canaanites, was known as the son of Dagon and the son of El. In Aria (Syria) he was called Hadad. He was a god of fertility, both of the womb and the land, providing life-giving rain. He was depicted as a standing bull, a popular symbol of fertility and strength. The worship of Baal involved temple prostitution and sometimes even child sacrifice. Ashtoreth was the female consort of Baal, associated with the evening star, a beautiful goddess of war and fertility. Later these characteristics were transferred by the Greeks to Aphrodite and by the Romans to Venus.
2:17	The covenant relationship with God had been violated and they gave themselves to other gods.
2:21-22	The Israelites failed this test of loyalty, see 3:5-6. They intermarried with the surrounding tribes with grave consequences, just as Joshua had warned (Joshua 23:12-13).

QUESTIONS

1. Why was it important that the Israelites should purge the land of its original inhabitants?

2. What were the results of their disobedience?

3. How does 2 Corinthians 6:14 link up with this passage in Judges and how does it apply to our Christian lives?

VISUAL AID

A map of the area (see page 83).

FOCUS ACTIVITY

Going Round in Circles Divide the group into 2 teams and ask each team to make a circle with the team members an arm length apart. No team member must touch another one. On the command to start, the leader of each team leaves their place, runs as quickly as possible around the outside of the circle without touching another team member and returns to where they started. If the runner touches anyone in the circle he/she must return to their place and start again.

When the runners arrives back where they started they touch the next person in the circle, who repeats the exercise. Continue until everyone in the circle has run. The first team to complete the exercise wins.

Talk about going round in circles. Did it achieve anything (apart from winning the game!). Over the next 5 sessions we will be looking at some people who kept going round in circles.

Photocopy page 84 for each group member.

Canaan in the Time of the Judges

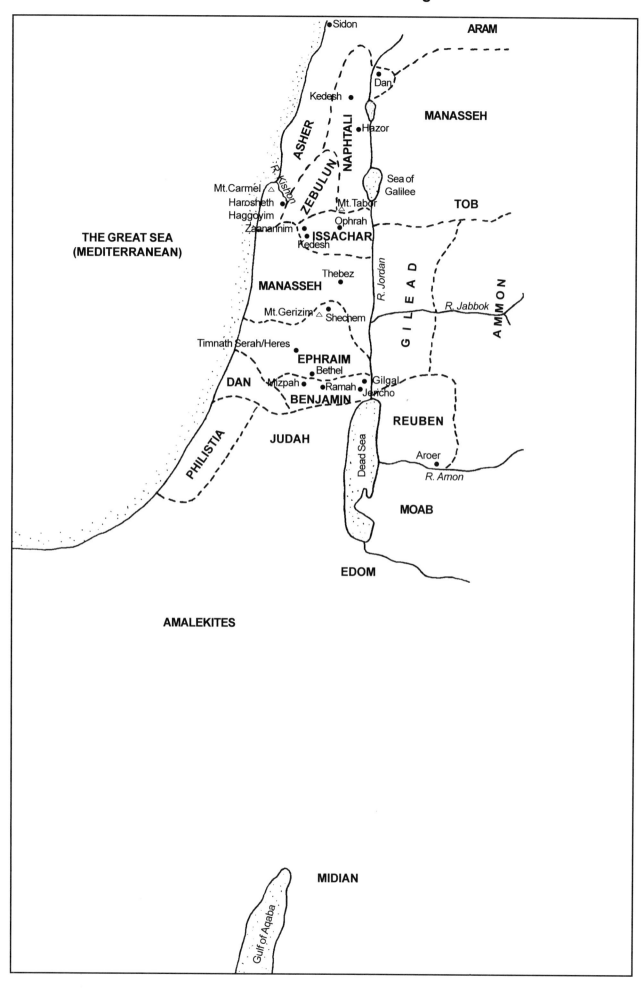

To summarise the situation during the time of the Judges start with the marked letter and trace the Bible verse through the maze. Each letter is used once only and you can move one letter at a time in any direction, including diagonally.

Now turn to the last chapter in Judges to see which verse this comes from?

Judges 21

PREPARATION

Judges 3:12-30

LESSON AIMS

To see the cyclic pattern of 'Judges' in operation.

3:12   Once again the Israelites did evil in the eyes of the Lord. This follows on from the previous 40 years of peace under Othniel, the first judge of Israel, (see 3:9-11).

3:12   Moab was a son/grandson of Lot (see Genesis 19:36-37). Lot had come with Abraham on his pilgrimage. He was a righteous man but had been compromised by the Sodomites. He and his daughters lived in a cave where Moab was conceived. He had not maintained the distinctiveness of Abraham. He had sown the 'seed of the flesh' and reaped its reward.

When the Israelites (Numbers 22) had been in the desert and very tired Balak king of Moab had used Balaam to cause the Israelites to eat food offered to idols and to commit immorality.

Isaiah 15 contains an oracle against Moab.

3:13   Ammonites were also descendants of Lot. see Genesis 19:38.

3:13   City of Palms - Jericho

3:15   'Left handed' - this was a feature of the Benjamites, (see 20:15-16), which was ironic as Benjamin means 'son of my right hand'. As he was left-handed Ehud could hide his sword on his right side, where it was not expected to be (see v.21).

'Tribute' - this was probably an annual payment, perhaps of some agricultural produce.

3:19   Ehud left the king's presence but at Gilgal turned back. The idols were carved stone images, possibly of Eglon himself, and were erected on the boundary of the territory that the king claimed as his own. The sight of these images may have prompted Ehud to return to the king.

3:20   Upper rooms were built on the flat roofs of houses and had latticed windows to provide a cool place in the summer.

3:28   Taking possession of the fords would prevent the Moabites from sending for reinforcements or escaping back to Jericho.

QUESTIONS

1. Ehud used his double-edged sword to execute judgment on Eglon. Look up Hebrews 4:12-13. How does God's word act as a sword?

2. From the cycle repeated several times in the book of Judges, summarise the details in this passage of:

     a)   disobedience

     b)   punishment

     c)   repentance

     d)   deliverance

A map of the area is useful (see page 83).

Left-handed Divide the group into teams. The teams form lines facing forwards. At the foot of the front person in each team place a number of objects, which can be transported using one hand, and a bucket. On the command to start, the person at the front of each team picks up an item with the left hand and passes it over his/her head to the person behind. The item is passed in this way from person to person until it reaches the end of the line. It is returned to the front by passing it between the team members' legs. Team members can **only** use their left hands. When the item reaches the front it is deposited in the bucket and the next item is passed down the line. The first team to complete the exercise wins.

Discuss the difficulty of using the left hand for those who are not naturally left-handed. Today's Bible study is about someone who found it an advantage to be left-handed.

Act out the story of Ehud. Divide the group in half and ask them to prepare a play from the passage to act to each other. The play can be either the Bible story or a modern adaptation. Each group is responsible for organising themselves. They should appoint a director, who can then decide with his/her group on the script, apportion parts, etc.

PREPARATION
Judges 4:1-24

LESSON AIMS

To see that God does not treat us as our sins deserve.

This chapter records Deborah's triumph over Sisera, the commander of the Canaanite army, and is followed by a celebration of the victory in chapter 5. At the time of these events Canaan was the only 'internal' enemy which Israel had; the other nations were outside the occupied territory.

4:3   They cried to the Lord for help, cf. Nehemiah 9:27.

4:4   Deborah means 'bee'. She is the only judge said to have been a prophet(ess). 'Leading' has traditionally been taken to mean judging.

4:6   Barak means 'thunderbolt'. His name occurs in the list of the faithful in Hebrews 11:32.

Kedesh in Naphtali was a town affected by the Canaanite oppression.

Mount Tabor is a mountain 1,300 feet high north east of the battle site.

4:7   With the Israelites encamped on Mount Tabor they would be safe from chariot attacks. Sisera's battle plan was clever - he chose to assemble in the Valley of Jezreel along the Kishon River, where he would have room to manoeuvre his troops and cover himself against attack from any quarter.

4:8-9   Barak's timidity is demonstrated here. He preferred to rely on Deborah rather than to trust in God for victory. See 9:54 - it was considered a disgrace to die at the hands of a woman.

4:11   Heber the Kenite - Heber can be translated as 'ally'. By stating that Heber had left the rest of his clan and moved closer to the Canaanites, the author is suggesting that Heber informed Sisera of Barak's military preparations.

4:15   'The Lord routed' - the Hebrew for routed is also used of the panic which overcame the Egyptians at the Red Sea (Exodus 14:24). In 5:20-21 Deborah praises the Lord for his power demonstrated in the storm and flood which caused the Canaanite downfall. Modern history has recorded similar flash floods in the Kishon River. In April 1799 Napoleon was assisted in his victory over the Turkish army by a similar storm.

4:18   'He entered her tent' - only the woman's father or husband had liberty to do that. This would, therefore, seem to be an ideal hiding place for Sisera.

4:19   'Skin' - a container for liquids made from goats' or lambs' skins.

4:21   Jael may have been an Israelite. In earlier generations the Kenites had allied themselves with the children of Israel, but her husband had deserted that previous alliance.

4:22-24   With Sisera dead the threat from Jabin had gone.

4:23   God subdued Jabin - the hand of God is seen in these events.

QUESTIONS

1. Did the Israelites deserve to be saved by Deborah under God's hand? What does the story show us about God and the way he deals with his people?

2. They cried to the Lord for help (4:3) and God answered them. Do we feel certain that God will answer our prayers when we cry for help? On what is this certainty based? See Psalm 34:15.

   NB Righteousness will need an explanation. Our righteousness in God's eyes is through the righteousness of the Lord Jesus, not earned by deed, cf. Romans 5:6-8.

3. God used Jael, a woman and a foreigner, to achieve his purpose. What does this teach us about God's sovereignty?

VISUAL AID

A map of the area is useful (see page 83).

FOCUS ACTIVITY

Rewards Before the activity starts, secretly hand out a small bar of chocolate or piece of fruit to 5 or 6 group members. Inform the group that there are 5/6 chocolate bars to be won during the activity. They must go round the room and shake everybody by the hand. The 5th person to shake the hand of a group member with a chocolate bar will be rewarded with that chocolate bar. (You might want to alter the number of handshakes required, depending on the number of players and the amount of time available.) Everyone plays the game, including those with the chocolate bars. (They should not know who are the other players with chocolate bars.) Players are allowed to shake a person's hand more than once, but not in the same encounter, (i.e. someone else must have shaken that person's hand before the first person returns to shake it again). The game finishes when all the chocolate bars have been won.

Talk about who was rewarded with chocolate bars and whether or not they deserved their reward. In today's Bible passage we will see whether or not God rewards us as we deserve.

ACTIVITY

Photocopy page 89 for each group member.

Unscramble each row of letters to make a five-lettered word. Having done that enter the words in the grid. You will then find that the central column, reading downwards, spells a word that describes Deborah.

EBHRE

KRAAB

NADST

DEVAS

TAGRE

PREPARATION

Judges 9:1-57

LESSON AIMS

To understand that, even though the times were evil, God was working out his purposes.

Abimelech was Gideon's (Jerub-Baal's) son born of a Canaanite concubine (see Judges 8:31). Gideon had rejected the Israelites' request to become king because he regarded the monarchy as usurping God's rule (Judges 8:22-23). In contrast with his father, Abimelech tried to set himself up as king with the help of Baal (9:4). In this and other respects he was the opposite of his father, who was one of the Lord's appointed judges. In the series overview Abimelech is listed as a judge, but if the definition of a judge was one 'whom God raised up to lead his people' then Abimelech cannot come into that category.

9:1	Shechem, at the foot of Mount Ebal, was the place where Abram had built an altar (Genesis 12:6-7). Jacob had dug a well on the site (Genesis 33:18) and this was where Jesus met and talked with the Samaritan woman (John 4:11). At the time of the judges it was a fortified city, probably associated with the temple of Baal-Berith, (see 9:4).
9:2	'Flesh and blood' - Abimelech was half Canaanite; he was hinting to the Shechemites that it might be better to be ruled by him rather than by total outsiders, i.e. Gideon's 70 sons.
9:4	'Reckless adventurers' - or hired mercenaries.
9:5	He slaughtered his half brothers like animals, almost as a coronation sacrifice.
9:6	'To crown Abimelech king' - the Canaanites had kings, in sharp contrast with the Israelites of the time.
9:8-15	The fable of the trees. The olive, fig tree and the vine were all plants of importance for their fruit. The thorn bush, by contrast, would produce nothing of value and would be a menace to farming - an apt metaphor for Abimelech.

Cedars of Lebanon symbolised the leading men of Shechem.

9:22	'Israel' - those in the area of Shechem who recognised Abimelech's authority.
9:23	'An evil spirit' - perhaps a spirit of bitterness and distrust.
9:26	'Put their confidence in him' - this shows the fickleness of the crowd, who changed their allegiance from Abimelech to Gaal.
9:27	The festival degenerated into a debauched drinking bout.
9:34	Four companies, or small contingents, would be better than one large one to avoid attention and to give greater freedom to attack from different directions.
9:45	'Scattered salt' - this symbolised perpetual bitterness and desolation.
9:49	Jotham's curse is fulfilled.
9:53	While men would be in the front line of attack with the weaponry of the time, women would help defend the town by dropping heavy stones on the attackers. The upper millstone was one of a pair of millstones with a circular hole in the middle, used for grinding corn. Abimelech was killed by a woman with a domestic implement - a double blow!!
9:56	'God repaid the wickedness' - God was in control of events, overruling the evil deeds of Abimelech.

QUESTIONS

1. Isaiah 40:15-17 tells us that God is in control of all the nations and events of the world. If you had lived during the 3 years of Abimelech's 'reign' why would it have been hard to believe that?

2. The judges were appointed by God; unlike the kings of the surrounding nations there was no dynastic succession. But, in his suggestion in verse 2, Abimelech acts as though there was. We all tend to be influenced by our culture. How can we determine what is right and how can we stand up to peer group pressure?

VISUAL AID

A map of the area is useful (see page 83)

FOCUS ACTIVITY

Who is in Control?   Divide the group into even-numbered teams. Each team divides into pairs, one to be the wheelbarrow and one to be the pusher. Mark out an obstacle course for the wheelbarrow pairs to negotiate. On the command to start, the first pair of each team completes the course as quickly as possible. Once the wheelbarrow reaches the finish line the next pair starts. The winning team is the first one to successfully complete the course.

Discuss who was in control - the wheelbarrow or the pusher? Was it easy negotiating the obstacles? Sometimes life can be like that and we seem to be out of control. In today's Bible passage we will see that God is always in control, even when it does not look like it.

ACTIVITY

Photocopy page 92 for each group member. The verse comes from Ecclesiastes 12:14

Fit the jigsaw pieces into the frame to discover what the Israelites needed to learn about God. Words are separated by 1 black square except at the end of each row. The black squares are included in the puzzle pieces. The black squares and starter letter in the frame should help you get started.

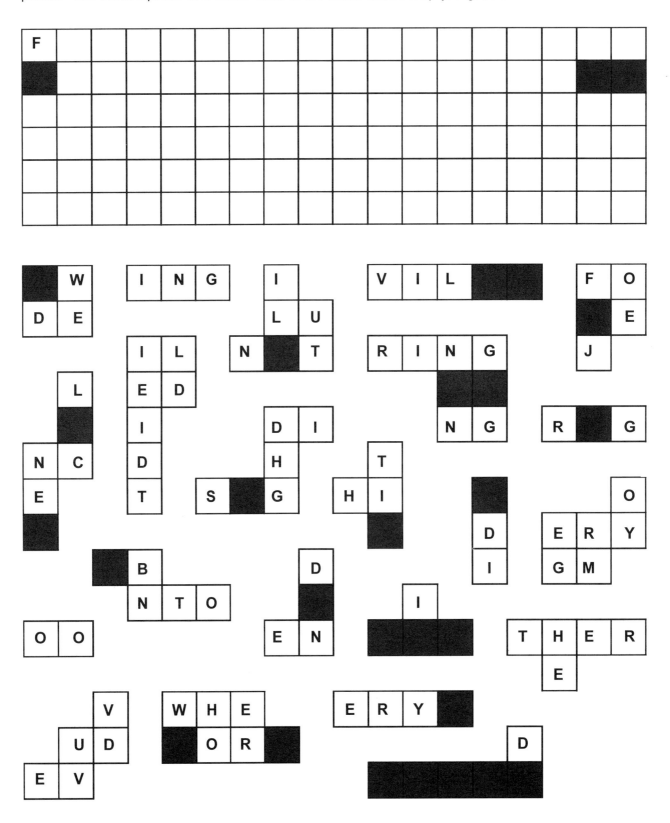

From where in the Bible does this verse come?

PREPARATION

Judges 10:6 - 12:7

LESSON AIMS

To learn the importance of words and that they can be used for good or evil.

10:6	Baal, Ashtoreth, gods of Aram - see Week 23 lesson notes.
	The gods of the Ammonites would include Molech, who was sometimes worshipped by offering human sacrifices, cf. 2 Kings 23:10.
10:16	Their repentance led to changed lives.
10:17	Mizpah means 'watchtower' and was a frequently used name at this time, e.g. Joshua 13:16 - Ramah Mizpah.
11:1	Jephthah's mother's prostitution would have given him the position of a social outcast, which was why he was driven away by his half brothers.
11:3	Tob is mentioned in 2 Samuel 10:6-8. The 'adventurers' were mercenaries.
11:8	The second offer to Jephthah came with the incentive that, after the fighting, he could be their regional leader.
11:11	His leadership was ratified in front of the people.
11:14 -27	Jephthah's diplomacy. His letter to the king of Ammon is a classic of its time. It reflects the prevailing thinking of that period that the god(s) of a nation established and protected their political boundaries and decided all disputes. Jephthah's claim to the land was threefold:

1. v.15-22 Israel had taken it from Sihon king of the Amorites, not from Ammon.

2. v.23-25 The Lord had given the land to Israel.

3. v.26-27 Israel had possessed the land for 300 years.

11:29	'The Spirit of the Lord' - see Judges 3:10; 6:34, etc. In OT times the empowering of the Holy Spirit was given

to individuals for specific tasks which God had given them to do. In the NT the Spirit is given to all believers at their conversion, (see Romans 8:9).

11:30	'Made a vow' - this was common practice among the Israelites, (see Genesis 28:20). There is an unresolved debate about the precise nature of the offering promised by Jephthah, but he probably had in mind a burnt offering of an animal.
11:35	He tore his clothes because he could not break his vow, (Numbers 30:2, Deuteronomy 23:21-23).
11:37	'I will never marry' - to be single and to have no children was a dreadful fate for an Israelite girl.
11:39	'Israelite custom' - this was probably a local one, as it is not mentioned anywhere else.
12:1	Ephraim - cf. Judges 8:1. Gideon had calmed down their resentment, but Jephthah confronted their anger after he had tried diplomacy. Ephraimites were descendants of Joseph. Jephthah was a descendant of Manasseh, therefore also descended from Joseph.
12:6	It appears that the Israelites east of the River Jordan pronounced the initial letters of Shibboleth with a strong 'sh' sound while those in Canaan gave it a softer 's' sound. So their accent betrayed their tribe.

QUESTIONS

1. Jephthah caused himself great distress by speaking unwisely. Look up James 3:1-12. What can we learn about the damage of hasty words?

2. Look up Proverbs 10:11; 16:23 and Ecclesiastes 5:2 These words are from the 'Wisdom Literature' section of the Bible. What can we learn about a person from what they say? On that basis how do you think you sound to people?

3. If you have any advice about 'keeping your mouth in check' pass it on to the group.

VISUAL AID

A map of the area is useful (see page 83).

FOCUS ACTIVITY

What happened next? Sit in a circle. The leader starts to tell a story. After a couple of sentences the leader claps his hands and the person sitting to his right takes up the story from where he left off. Every few sentences the leader claps his hands and the next person must continue the story. Keep going until the story comes round to the leader, who finishes it off. Players have to keep going with no hesitations. Anyone, who hesitates, is out.

Using episodes from the 'story', discuss what happens when people speak without thinking. Today's Bible passage is about someone who spoke without thinking, with tragic results.

ACTIVITY

Photocopy page 95 for each group member.

Judges Alphabet

The answer to each question begins with the given letter of the alphabet. Try to answer the questions without looking up the Bible verses; these are given to help you if you get stuck.

A..................................... A Judge but not a Judge (9:1-3)

B..................................... A pagan god (2:11)

C..................................... The land given to the Children of Israel

D..................................... A female Judge (4:4)

E..................................... Another Judge (3:15)

F..................................... A descriptive word for the king of Moab (3:17)

G..................................... Where Jephthah came from (11:1)

H..................................... The husband of Jael (4:17)

I..................................... The name of God's people

J..................................... The king of Canaan (4:2)

K..................................... Heber was from this tribe (4:11)

L..................................... A descriptive word for Ehud (3:15)

M..................................... An enemy of Israel (3:12)

N..................................... The name of Joshua's father (2:8)

O..................................... The type of tree referred to in Jotham's story (9:8)

P..................................... Enemies of Israel (10:7)

Q..................................... Abimilech's order to his men (9:48)

R..................................... Near where Deborah held court (4:5)

S..................................... He was killed by a tent peg (4:21)

T..................................... The type of bush in Jotham's story (9:14)

U..................................... What was dropped on Abimilech (9:53)

V..................................... God gave this to Jephthah (12:3)

W..................................... What Sisera asked Jael for (4:19)

X..................................... The number of years Israel was subject in Roman numerals (4:3)

Y..................................... Each year these commemorate Jephthah's daughter (11:40)

Z..................................... A governor of Shechem (9:30)

Syllabus for On The Way for 11-14s

Book 1 (28 weeks)		Book 3 (28 weeks)		Book 5 (26 weeks)	
Abraham	(7)	Joseph	(7)	Bible Overview	(26)
Jacob	(7)	People in Prayer	(7)		
The Messiah (Christmas)	(2)	The Saviour of the World (Christmas)	(3)		
Jesus said, 'I am …'	(7)	Is God Fair? (Predestination)	(2)		
Ruth	(5)	Learning from a Sermon	(3)		
		The Sermon on the Mount	(6)		

Book 2 (25 weeks)		Book 4 (25 weeks)		Book 6 (27 weeks)	
Rescue (Easter)	(3)	Psalms (Easter)	(2)	A Selection of Psalms	(5)
Paul (Acts 9-16)	(7)	Paul's Latter Ministry	(7)	The Normal Christian Life	(7)
Philippians	(5)	Colossians	(5)	Revelation	(9)
Paul (Acts 17-18)	(3)	Choose Life (Hell & Judgment)	(2)	Homosexuality	(1)
1 Thessalonians	(6)	The Kings	(9)	The Dark Days of the Judges	(5)
Suffering	(1)				

The books can be used in any order.

The number in brackets indicates the number of lessons in a series.

For more information about *On the Way for 11-14s* please contact:
Christian Focus Publications, Fearn, Tain, Ross-shire, IV20 1TW / Tel: +44 (0) 1862 871 011 or
TnT Ministries, 29 Buxton Gardens, Acton, London, W3 9LE / Tel: +44 (0) 20 8992 0450

CHRISTIAN FOCUS
Good books with the real message of hope!

Christian Focus Publications publishes biblically-accurate books for adults and children. If you are looking for quality Bible teaching for children then we have a wide and excellent range of Bible story books - from board books to teenage fiction, we have it covered. You can also try our new Bible teaching Syllabus for 3-9 year olds and teaching materials for pre-school children. These children's books are bright, fun and full of biblical truth, an ideal way to help children discover Jesus Christ for themselves. Our aim is to help children find out about God and get them enthusiastic about reading the Bible, now and later in their lives. Find us at our web page: www.christianfocus.com

TnT Ministries

TnT Ministries (which stands for Teaching and Training Ministries) was launched in February 1993 by Christians from a broad variety of denominational backgrounds who were concerned that teaching the Bible to children be taken seriously. The leaders were in charge of the Sunday School of 50 teachers at St Helen's Bishopsgate, an evangelical church in the City of London, for 13 years, during which time a range of Biblical teaching materials was developed. TnT Ministries also runs training days for Sunday School teachers.